Game, Set, Match

BOOKS BY

Charlie Jones and Kim Doren

You Go Girl!:
Winning the Woman's Way

You Go Girl!:
A Journal to Get You There

Be the Ball:
A Golf Instruction Book for the Mind

That's Outside My Boat:
Letting Go of What You Can't Control

BY Charlie Jones

What Makes Winners Win

Game, Set, Match

A Tennis
Book
for the Mind

Charlie Jones
and
Kim Doren

**Andrews McMeel
Publishing**

Kansas City

Interior page design by Pete Lippincott

02 03 04 05 06 QUF 10 9 8 7 6 5 4 3 2 1

Library of Congress Cataloging-in-Publication Data

Jones, Charlie, 1930–
     Game, set, match : a tennis book for the mind / Charlie Jones and Kim Doren.
          p. cm.
     ISBN 0-7407-2219-0
          1. Tennis—Psychological aspects. I. Doren, Kim. II. Title.

GV1002.9.P75 J66 2002
796.342'01'9—dc21   2002018350

ATTENTION: SCHOOLS AND BUSINESSES

Andrews McMeel books are available at quantity discounts with bulk purchase for educational, business, or sales promotional use. For information, please write to: Special Sales Department, Andrews McMeel Publishing, 4520 Main Street, Kansas City, Missouri 64111.

To Chuck and Julie.

*If I could have chosen
from all the children in the world,
I would have chosen you.*

—CHARLIE

To Barb (Mom),

*for showing me that in life,
unlike tennis,
love is the only score that counts.
(Just don't tell that to her weekly tennis group—
Ann Marie, Helen, Judy, and Patsy!)*

—KIM

"From what we get, we can make a living; what we give, however, makes a life."

—ARTHUR ASHE,
champion

Contents

Foreword

In tennis, the mind often gets in the way of the body. That is obvious to anyone who has ever played. In a practice session, you may hit the ball unbelievably well; then in a match, you become a completely different person. What happens? It's your mind. Your mind just won't leave you alone. You have to calm your mind to be able to have that same feeling you have when you're hitting the ball great in a practice session. The sooner you can accomplish this, the better you are going to perform in a match.

Some people have spectacular talent, but they just can't pull it off during a match. Others have limited talent, but they get more out of their ability. The mind is what separates the two. Players go from being tremendously confident to tremendously unconfident. You see it all the time. That's why *Game, Set, Match* is such an important tennis book. It shows you how to improve your mind-set, and when you do that, you'll elevate your game.

—STAN SMITH

CHAPTER ONE

The Mind Game

"Champions have a different mental state than others."

—VENUS WILLIAMS,
U.S. Open and Wimbledon champion

Gene Scott

Founder and publisher of Tennis Week *magazine
and columnist for the* Moscow News

You start out with the premise and the obvious fact that tennis is a game of boring repetitions. The person at first blush who's the most successful is the person who can hit the ball the most times over the net over the same rectangle in a row without making a mistake. That by itself is sort of a metronomic tedium and there's no other sport like it. There's no variety whatsoever. The variety all comes from the mind. What can I do with this boring metronome that can add some spice to an otherwise tedious game from its very diagram?

The game is played in 201 nations, so you have at least 201 varieties of forehands and the same number of strange backhands and serves and overheads. So from the variety of styles of play, you get this incredible tapestry of different types of strokes. And you also see how successfully someone can execute all of this variety of play over this boring rectangle. It's only in the improvisation of the mind that you can bring any variety to the game at all. That's the basic precept.

Let's say you have two people who are exactly equally matched; they have the same serve, same volley, same foot speed. Who wins? Naturally, it's the player who's the toughest mentally, the player who finds a way to be mentally stronger than his opponent. It's not merely a matter of bringing variety into your strokes because the rectangle is boring. It's a mental challenge to find a way to out-tough your opponent even though your styles are equally matched. You must bring variety to a game that imposes a lack of variety and you must also be unbelievably mentally tough in a situation where you don't have any support from a teammate or from any natural barrier in the court that could give you an advantage.

In tennis, basically everybody has the same rectangle, so you have to figure out a way to outlast your opponent by perseverance. If he has the same perseverance dynamic that you have, then you need to say, "What else can I do?" Everybody can hit a winner sometimes. What matters is who can do it better in multiple repetitions. That is what will determine the outcome.

"Whatever happens, happens. I can't control the play of other players. I can just play my game."

—LINDSAY DAVENPORT,
ranked number one worldwide in 2001

Jack Kramer

Great player, exceptional promoter, thoughtful innovator, and astute television commentator

It's obvious that all players have a certain amount of equipment and strokes, and hopefully a good serve. But where the mind comes in is how to use what you've got. You have to have a mind that tells you when you shouldn't try to do too much. You can only put the ball away from certain positions on the court. The people with the good minds never seem to try to make the big shot if it can't produce a winner, so they cut down their errors. I think that's one of the big decisions; the mind helps make winners win.

I don't know what goes through Pete Sampras's mind. He's a great player, but he has this habit: He wants to use his big weapon, which is his forehand, all the time. He has a mind that says, "Go for it, Pete," from deep positions. When you're a couple feet behind the baseline and your opponent is in the back court, the chances of you knocking off a winner are maybe fifty to one. It's the one big weakness that he has and it has to come from his mind.

The easiest place to put the ball away is at the net when it's a high ball, so you can volley it away. Progressively going away from the net, you should be able to go for a winner with any ball that's inside the service line that is anywhere near the height of the net. Back toward the baseline another six feet, it's according to the height of the bounce: The higher the bounce, the easier it is for you to hit an angle, and if you hit it hard enough, it should be a winner. When you're approaching the baseline, the chances of knocking that ball off are pretty slim. You really should play that ball safe and as deep as possible.

The people who win in tennis find a way to make their opponents make a mistake, an unforced error. Sometimes it's just the threat of a big serve. When Sampras is serving, for instance, the opponent on defense realizes that if he doesn't do something really good with the return, Pete is probably going to knock the next one off. The opponents make a lot of errors just making sure that Pete doesn't make a placement.

A lot of people are losing because they're giving their opponents too much credit. What they should do is make their opponents keep the ball in play. Even though they may not be the best players, they should remember that some-times the best player tries to play too well and he makes mistakes and loses.

Your mind should always be working—according to the score of the game and to who's serving—as to what you are going to do on the next shot. The key to tennis is holding your serve when you're down a break point. On the other side, when you get up a break point, that's the time when you want to make sure you don't miss it, just in case you can get your opponent to make a mistake. Those are the periods where your mind should be working very fast to make sure you are in charge of your serve, as that's the one time where you can do anything you want with the ball.

When the other player is serving on those big points, you've really got to get your mind working. Know the percentages of where he's going to serve. If you've got a weak backhand, it helps you because your mind says, "Most probably he's going to come to my backhand." What you can prepare yourself for is what you're going to do if your mind is right on the percentages.

When the crunch is on, you want to play to your opponent's weakness. You try to gear your mind to thinking in that direction. You also anticipate that by playing to the person's weakness, he's probably going to hit the ball in a certain area, so you want to make sure you're heading toward that area. Those are the kinds of things the winners' minds produce at the right time.

"Your mind goes along with your base tennis. If you've worked and have confidence in your ground strokes and your game, and if you've worked hard enough to develop something that's dependable, then you can use your brain a little more."

—LOUISE BROUGH CLAPP,
winner of thirty-five Grand Slam tennis titles

"Winning is a lot of things. It's strategy and technique and concentration and fight. It's all about figuring out how to beat your opponent."

—DODO CHENEY,
winner of more than 300 national tennis titles

Ted Schroeder
Wimbledon and U.S. singles champion

Tennis is a game of percentages, pure and simple. When you're playing a serve-and-volley game, there are three things that can happen and two of them are good for you—that's better than the house gets at Las Vegas. The old axiom is "The more you hang around Vegas, the more certain you are to go Tap City." The same thing is true with a good volleyer against a good net player. In the end, the percentage is finally going to get you.

The only mind game in tennis is when you play a good player. All the good players understand the angles: the high and low spots of the net, the long and short dimensions of the court. For example, you've got 6.2 feet longer to lob by going cross-court. For every shot, there is the automatic-reflex reply. For every reply, there is a classic reply to the reply. And so on and so on. It comes down to a matter of execution.

The only mind game is to understand what the other player is going to do. Frank Parker had a very bad forehand. Jack Kramer and I beat him unmercifully. It was reasonably close, but he never won a match against us. We'd play him the same as we played everybody else. We'd attack. When we'd play a volley, in any match, unless it was a winning shot, we'd play it a little bit to the backhand side of the center of the court on the guy's backhand. With Parker, we did the same thing, even though he had as good a backhand as Ken Rosewall or Don Budge.

The reporters used to ask us, "Why do you keep playing to Parker's backhand?" The answer was very simple: Because he had to make the proper shot. We knew what he was going to try. Whereas if we hit it to his forehand, particularly on a critical point, he was going to almost miss it or hit it on the wood or do something crazy with it. The more critical the point was, the surer it was that we would hit to his backhand, because we knew what he was going to try to do. With a couple of exceptions, none of the guys playing the game today understands this.

"The mind game is really not what you know; it's what the players who should be greater players because of what they don't know, won't take the time and trouble to learn."

—TED SCHROEDER

"The biggest thing is to look into yourself and find out who you are. Once you're really not afraid to find out who you are and tap into whatever your strengths are, you are very capable of being successful in whatever you want to do. There are a lot of times that we don't really want to look at who we are."

—ZINA GARRISON,
first African American woman to play in a major final (1990 Wimbledon) since Althea Gibson won Wimbledon in 1958

Vic Braden

Psychologist, sports researcher, and tennis
coach for fifty-seven years

I was playing Bobby Riggs in the Cleveland Arena and I was ahead 4–1 in the first set. This was the first time I'd ever had a chance to find out whether I might be able to play with the big boys and I was killing him on the backhand side. Well, Bobby knew all this stuff that psychologists have found out since. He knew it forty years ago.

On the changeover, he walked right up to me and said, "Hang in there; your backhand will come back." I started thinking about my backhand and about how crazy he was and I lost it. I lost the match. That's the mind game. He knew I would be thinking about what he said. That's what winners do. They find some way to win. Losers find some way, if they hang in there long enough, to lose.

"You've got to give your opponent an opportunity to find a way to lose."

—VIC BRADEN

"You have to have the ability to tune everything out."

—CHRIS EVERT,
winner of six U.S. Open championships

"I got that mental, physical, and emotional high because I loved what I was doing. I had a passion for it and when those came together in certain matches, there was no better feeling in life."

—CHRIS EVERT

"Work hard while you're on the court and stay in the moment. Just concentrate and work on your game. Once you're off the court, don't dwell on things, especially if you lost the match. Family and education are more important. Tennis is a game."

—CHRIS EVERT

Stan Smith

U.S. Open and Wimbledon champion

First of all, the mind game is pretty complicated because of all the different strategies involved. If you're playing somebody and you don't have an idea of what your game plan should be, then you won't have the confidence to hit the ball the way you should.

I realize there are a lot of different ways to be successful as far as technique in hitting the ball. If you compare the games of John McEnroe, Jimmy Connors, Bjorn Borg, and Pete Sampras, you see a lot of different styles of hitting the ball. Jim Courier is a perfect example. His backhand is very unusual. When looking at him as a kid, you might have said that he didn't have it because he has an unusual technique. That was also said about Borg's forehand, before the semi-Western forehand was popular.

For the top players, the difference is in the mind. They're able to assimilate information very quickly—not only very quickly during a point, but in general. All the players I just mentioned were not overly coached and therefore they had to figure it out themselves. They're fairly independent on the court and they did it because of their minds.

The one thing that is hard to describe and calculate is how much the experience of being there helps you. It's not only the actual play itself, but also handling the press, handling the expectations of the press, your peers, the coaches who are helping you, and yourself—knowing what it's like to be in that situation. Until you're there, you're not sure what it's like; you're uncertain.

Uncertainty may be the biggest word that affects players. It can separate players at the highest level because the very top players have been successful at Wimbledon or at the U.S. Open. There's always some uncertainty, but when the top players get in tight situations, they really come through when it counts. They hit a big shot when it counts or they play the right percentage when it counts. They make the right decisions and they're able to execute them.

A lot of people can make the right decisions, but they're not capable of executing. That's where having confidence in yourself comes into play. When I was in the finals at Wimbledon the second year, I'd been there before. I knew what the feeling was going to be walking onto Centre Court, how to bow to the royal box, and I expected to win, unlike the year before.

That second year, the final was rained out for the first time ever at Wimbledon. It never even started. It was totally canceled that day. This circumstance probably helped me, because the year before at the U.S. Open when I won, my semifinal match was rained out three days in a row. In both cases, I went into the final thinking I could win and I should win. My mind-set was very positive. I thought I was going to win Wimbledon. Ultimately, that would make a big difference. I did win.

"I was always second. The people respect me, but second place is not good enough. Finally, I am a champion of Wimbledon. Whatever I do in my life, wherever I go, I am always going to be a Wimbledon champion."

—GORAN IVANISEVIC,
after winning the 2001 Wimbledon championship

"In sports, the more you can stay inside yourself the more chance you have to win or to be successful. As soon as you start dealing with the player on the other side of the net, you've got a big problem."

—AHMAD RASHAD,
former all-pro wide receiver for the
Minnesota Vikings and tennis buff

Regis Philbin

Host of Live with Regis and Kelly *and*
Who Wants to Be a Millionaire

A mind game? You're asking the right guy. Sometimes I get so depressed when I miss a shot. I get so furious and suddenly it's over. The other guy wins and I get even more pissed off! A lot of people are affected like that. I admire the pros. I watch them closely, like Pete Sampras and Andre Agassi. When they miss a shot, boy, there's no sign of any hurt. They just go about their business and get ready for the next shot.

Me, I'm throwing rackets, I'm breaking rackets. So you've got the wrong guy if you want to know how to overcome frustration. I know how to get it; I don't know how to overcome it. All I know is the anguish. Send me this book when you're finished, because I still don't know how to handle that.

Tennis really is a head game. About thirty years ago, I was playing tennis at ABC director Andy Sidaris's place in Truesdale. I threw my racket after I missed a shot and it ended up on the roof of the house next door. To this day, you can still see my racket sitting up there on the roof. For thirty years, it has put up with the rain, the wind, the birds, and everything else.

I play a lot of doubles with my wife and if that isn't a marriage killer, I don't know what is. It's very dangerous because I have a tendency to slough it off and say it's her fault even though I missed the shot. All the little past experiences come up and it's not too good for the marriage and it's even worse for my tennis game.

I can be sensational for a set. But if we take a layoff before the next set—if we cool off, just sit down for a minute, take a sip of water, talk for a second—my game's gone. I cannot get it back. Conversely, if I lose, I make it a point to say, "Let's sit down for a second." I want my opponent to cool off. By and large, it works. The winner can't seem to win that second set after they cool off. The interruption is enough to throw off their mind-set. I have found that to be the rule, so I always do it.

"I need to shout, or I need to throw the racket. Otherwise, it's difficult to play, because you get very nervous each time. Sometimes it works; sometimes no. But normally it works."

—MARAT SAFIN,
2000 U.S. Open champion

"When you throw the racket, you throw the racket. I mean, you break it. You have to smack it, to get angry."

—GORAN IVANISEVIC,
2001 Wimbledon champion

"I used to see people blow up on the tennis court. They'd get so mad, they'd throw their rackets. They'd be upset about something and then it'd take them seven or eight points to get over it. I always thought that those emotional outbursts wasted way too much energy."

—AHMAD RASHAD,
former all-pro wide receiver for the Minnesota Vikings and tennis buff

Bud Collins

Tennis writer for the Boston Globe *and colorful
television commentator*

Tennis is almost like boxing in that you're trying to do
something to disrupt your opponent. You're all alone.
The mind part means you can get very nervous. You can
choke much easier than in a team game, where you have
your comrades inspiring you. There's no bench. If it's in the
fifth set and you're thinking, "Geez, I'm worn out," you
have to build yourself up mentally. You still have to play the
fifth set.

There are so many instances in which the mind comes
into play, where perhaps in a team game it wouldn't. In a
team game, if you're worn out, they take you out. If you're
looking a little shaky, they take you out. If you're looking a
little shaky, your teammates might kick you in the butt and
say, "We can do it." There's nobody to do that on a tennis
court. It's just you. It comes down to you. It's athletic chess,
and you're making all the moves.

I don't know if the mind is as important now as it once
was. Power has taken over so much that a lot of the tennis is
mindless. It's just hit it as hard as you can and hope it doesn't
come back. So far, the women haven't quite overpowered
the game the way the men have, and I think that's probably
why women are in the spotlight these days. Their game is
more interesting.

For instance, their best surface is grass. So the women at Wimbledon are just sensational. They can bring all their strokes to bear, they can get to the net, and they don't get caught up in dull rallies like they do on clay because the grass won't permit that. They show off their best at Wimbledon.

On the other hand, grass is the worst surface for men. Even though in 2001 fans were saying the final was one of the greatest matches of all times, it wasn't! It was still two-shot tennis, but there was drama in the fact that Goran Ivanisevic, the unexpected finalist, the real long shot, was playing Patrick Rafter. But it was two- and three-shot tennis. Serve and volley; you return or you don't. In this case, it took on great drama, but the semifinal match with Patrick Rafter and Andre Agassi was far better.

Tennis is still a sport in which the mind really has a lot to do with the outcome. For example, consider the choking that happens when you don't do your best when you need to, or, conversely, when you play like a champion when you have to play like a champion.

The problem with the present game is that the rackets need to be changed. You can't go back to wood; the craftsmen don't exist and nobody would want to do that. But I've talked to scientists at MIT and they tell me they could take a lot of power away from the rackets by removing some of the titanium or graphite. Also, I think a critical thing is to bring the racket back down to size. When I started playing, the rackets were no longer than twenty-seven inches or wider than nine inches. Remember when you could measure the net with two rackets?

You don't see a lot of tennis artistry anymore because of the overhitting. I think they should develop a formula in professional tennis for the racket so that it is depowered. Have a disarmament conference. You'd bring back touch to the game.

There are more good players now than ever before. I don't know that the greats are any greater. I think if Bill Tilden came around, he'd find a way to win. But tennis would be more interesting if it wasn't so based on power, because it takes a lot of fun out of it for the spectators. Without the spectators, you can go home and play in your backyard.

———————————

"I love playing tennis; I love winning titles. And I realized I wouldn't be any happier in my life in general if I won or lost. Sure, in the tennis part of my life, I'd be much happier. But winning, losing, money, riches, or fame don't make you happy. For my tennis career, this is great. But as far as being Venus, it doesn't really make a huge difference."

—VENUS WILLIAMS,
U.S. Open and Wimbledon champion

"I always wanted to be number one from the time I was little. That was always my dream. I love playing on the big courts with all the fans. But I knew that it would take a lot of work to get there. I wanted to put in all the hours and learn from my mistakes so I could get better and become the best player in the world."

—SERENA WILLIAMS,
U.S. Open champion

"I believe the best training you can get is inside your head."

—RICHARD WILLIAMS,
father of tennis stars Venus and Serena

Mary Carillo

Winner of the French Open mixed-doubles title
with John McEnroe

Tennis is a mind game. That is the joy of it and that is the curse of it. It's like what Yogi Berra said, "Ninety percent of baseball is 50 percent mental," or whatever it was he said. If all you needed was a big old swing and a nice fastball serve, a lot of people could play tennis successfully for a long time.

There's not much hitting involved in the actual game. There's running and there's some striking of the ball, and then there are changeovers where you get to relive your entire career for ninety seconds. That used to happen to me in the middle of a match.

I was a good thinking player, but unfortunately I had such limited skills that I'd be ready to hit my backhand at some key moment in the match and I'd be thinking about what I could do right now with a huge topspin-forehand cross-court winner. Then I'd do this total scallop, chicken, bologna, and cheese chip backhand that went nowhere and I'd be picked off at the net. It's such a mental game.

One of the big problems is that there's still no coaching allowed. Another problem is that there are no substitutes. You can't take yourself out or have someone take you out when you have nowhere to go. There's no clock that runs out so that mercifully the match is over. This means you could be up a set at 5–1 and forty-five minutes later you've lost the stinker.

There are all these things that weigh upon you. Some points are worth a lot more than others. Some are really expensively lost points. Some are weighted so much in terms of breaking someone's serve or breaking your own heart. That's when I always choked. I'd be thinking, "This must be a big point because I can't move my elbow!"

I always loved watching Jimmy Connors and Andre Agassi. They could be losing and they'd still be trying to find their way and they'd still be getting out hit. Then all of a sudden, they would hit one screaming forehand down-the-line-winner and they'd immediately think they could win the match. They're down a set and a break and they'd hit one shot and it'd be worth twenty-seven points, not just one. They get this rush and they know they're still very much in the match. Their opponent sees that and they quail a little bit. The entire psychology of the match would change on one point.

I also saw Martina Navratilova when she was up a set and two breaks and yet she figured out a way to lose that match. Ted Tinling watched the same match. Martina was preposterously up on somebody at the U.S. Open—in the semis, I believe it was—and suddenly she went away. I went up to Ted after the match and I was shaking my head, because I'd broadcast it. I said, "Ted, why?" Ted, in that gorgeous voice of his, said, "Once again, Martina saw vultures that no one else could see." Isn't that great? And you do; that happens.

The Mind Game

The people who can really stay on their side of the court and inside their own heads tend to do better in those big moments. They're the thinkers. There are bangers who are very tough to play, but it's the thinkers who know how to take down the bangers. The thinkers figure out a way.

I love watching a match where a really good thinking player is going down and you can almost see them stop themselves. Walking over to a changeover, you can almost feel them cogitating and you know they're thinking to themselves, "There has to be a way I can win this match." Most other players go into the changeover thinking, "This sucks; I'm blowing it." They're sucking and blowing at the same time, which is physiologically impossible. Those thinkers are the ones who stick around and win the trophy.

"Billie Jean King's biggest mantra is 'Champions adjust.' Champions know how to figure out a way to win."

—MARY CARILLO

"Mentally, when I was concentrating, it was just like meditation. I've meditated every day of my life just by being on the tennis court. That's what concentration is. It's meditating."

—CHRIS EVERT,
seven-time French Open champion

Randy Snow

Winner of ten U.S. Open wheelchair tennis championships

I like to say that a disability resulting from a traumatic accident is just like your freshman year in college. You're going to be weeded out. If you have processes that can allow you to deal with change and you can refocus and redeem and move forward, you can become a tennis player. A lot of people have these injuries and they don't make it into the sport.

Wheelchair tennis is not for the people who need it; it's for the people who want it. The people who play are the ones who survive. That trickles over into the game because life is about surviving and problem solving. You still have people who play the victim in their tennis game in our sport, just like they would if they were able-bodied. Sport is about success and failure and endurance. Our sport is no different. Wheelchair tennis is just a microcosm of all sports.

The beauty of our wheelchair sport is how it can be presented. There are basically three theaters. First is the rehabilitative theater. That's when you're injured and in rehab and you're asked to participate in a wheelchair tennis clinic. That's therapy. It allows you to forget about the adversity and the challenge and have some fun, so it's rehabilitative.

Next is the recreational theater. This happens after you're discharged from the hospital. You go home and you're in your community. You've accepted your disability, returned to work; you're with your family and you want to play tennis. Now wheelchair tennis is recreational. You go play and enjoy the game.

Following this is the competitive theater. There are varying levels, but to play in the U.S. Open, the highest level, is very difficult. It's quite an accomplishment. You go to sleep thinking about your game and the first thing you do when you wake up is you revisit it. It's always on your mind.

I lived the game. I videotaped all my opponents. I'd play my match, then tape the next person I was going to play, and that night, I'd watch those tapes. Everything I did was focused on my goal of winning the U.S. Open. It just never ended. When Isaac Newton was interviewed about the law of gravity, they asked him, "How did you do this?" He said, "I thought about it all the time!" That's exactly what you need to do if you want to win the U.S. Open. You've got to live the U.S. Open. It's no different for Michael Dell or Donald Trump or Pete Sampras.

People, and this applies to able-bodied players as well, don't practice the mental part of the game. They'll go out and work their butt off for hours and days and years, but what are they reading at night? Are they practicing focus techniques away from the sport? Are they doing difficult things in their lives that build a mental edge? That's what it takes.

Maybe it's giving up a certain food or confronting your father with whom you've had issues your entire life, or asking a gal to marry you, or parachuting. Perhaps it's reading about other people who have overcome challenges. I don't believe that athletes do that very much. Mental practicing that occurs off the court is essential. When you arrive at a tournament and you have your practice techniques in place, you're comfortable. You can tap into those things.

I don't think there's any difference with able-bodied athletes or wheelchair athletes. I did the work. I visualized. I got up in the morning and I said, "I'm the winner of the gold medal in Barcelona at the Paralympics." I started saying that months before the Games. And when I went to bed I said the same thing. I had a positive affirmation stuck on my mirror so I could see it every morning. I believe in the mental edge. To do it, you've got to do it for a long time, and then it's familiar and it becomes a habit.

You've got a lot of able-bodied players who are trying to be the champion. But are they doing the right type of work? They all train hard. They train all day long. But do they do the mental part? I believe the mental aspect takes practice.

"It's not about U.S. Open championships; it's about what you learn about yourself. It's setting a goal, designing a plan, pursuing it, dealing with failure, making adjustments, and then going home after you've lost and saying to yourself, as John Maxwell said, 'It's not about the success; it's about what you do after the failure.' Wheelchair tennis offers that venue."

—RANDY SNOW

"I don't play wheelchair singles any more because I'm not letting those kids hammer on a U.S. Open champion and then go around the tournament grounds and tell everybody. I'm not letting them do that. I may be forty-two years old, but my little-boy ego is hugely raging inside of me."

—RANDY SNOW

Geoff Griffin

Director of the Balboa Tennis Club in San Diego

The USTA has now adopted a rule that wheelchair players are allowed to play in all tournaments. They can enter any tournament. The Tournament Director has to decide where to put them.

A couple of wheelchair players played in our district tournament last year. One of them was an A player and we let him play in the Cs. He won two rounds before he lost in the third.

They get the two bounces, but other than that, the rules are the same. It worked pretty well. One of the able-bodied players was upset that he lost, but I think it was just an ego thing.

"The physical challenge that a wheelchair-tennis player faces is the same as any athlete. I don't care if you're standing up or you're sitting down. If you have a passion or a desire to compete, you're going to train, prepare, eat, sleep, and do whatever it may take to get you to the level that you want to be on the tennis court and in the rankings. I don't think this is unique to the individual with a disability."

—RICK DRANEY,
*six-time U.S. Open wheelchair-tennis champion
(quad division)*

CHAPTER TWO

The Will to Win

"Only the strong survive."

—JENNIFER CAPRIATI,
2001 and 2002 Australian Open champion

Tony Trabert

Winner of French, Wimbledon, and U.S. singles titles

First of all, you're playing directly against somebody. It's not like golf, where you're playing the course. You are *mano a mano*. That's part of why it's a mind game. The veteran players, the top pros, don't have that problem because they were jerked around when they were younger, when they were learning. Everybody says, "We can psyche you out." But you're not going to psyche out any of the top guys.

When you know you've prepared yourself as well as you can off the court, you know you can stay out there forever. A lot of people don't want to do that. That becomes the mind game. They look at you, it's the middle of the fifth set, it's hot, you're tired, they're tired, and they think, "Man, this guy's never going to quit; he's never going to run down." So they just get out as fast as they can and go home. This is all part of your mind game, your will to win. Because you're playing against another human being, the mind has a great deal to do with it.

I never felt safe until I got in the locker room, where nothing else bad could happen. I've never understood why you can't go out there and concentrate. You're there because you want to be there. It's the only game in town at the moment; there's nothing else going on. Why not pay attention and grind?

The Will to Win

I won the U.S. championships twice and Wimbledon without losing a set, and I had the ability to get to a pretty good level and stay there. When you practice and you know you can play pretty well, you know not to try low percentage stuff in big points. That's all part of concentration. You know when to play the percentage shots, when to play your best stuff, and when to gamble a little bit.

Some of the kids who play today don't recognize that all the points don't have the same value. They play a love–40 point the same as they play a 40–love point, and that's not necessarily the way to play this game. When you get break points, you need to play a little differently than you would if you're up 40–love.

My viewpoint as a player was if I had somebody down love–40 on his serve, I would play the first point as a good percentage point and not try some screwy thing. If they won the point, I might be able to gamble the second point, and if that didn't work, then I'd play a good solid percentage-type point on the third point. I'm playing two of those three points by the book. I don't mean safe, but I'm not trying something flaky that's not going to work for me.

I see players who have 40–love on their serve and they serve a second serve as hard as the first serve and double-fault. Nobody thinks much about it. They miss a volley, they get passed, and suddenly it's deuce. Their lead evaporates and they end up losing. That's all part of the will to win.

"You have to have the mentality of executing your game when you don't feel like there's a lot of hope. By the same token, you also need a lot of luck. Sometimes they come together."

—ANDRE AGASSI,
winner of all four Grand Slam titles

"I'm not sure if in the past I believed in my game as much as I do now. Now I'm out on the court feeling like I'm going to make somebody beat me. It's always a good feeling when you are out there focused on making it a miserable day for your opponent."

—ANDRE AGASSI

"Andre Agassi still thinks he can get better. When I hear that from a guy as great as he is, then I know that's what sports is all about."

—LARRY STEFANKI,
tennis coach to the pros

Dick Gould

Stanford University tennis coach

Tennis is actually a very simple game, but people make it in their minds much more complex than it really is. You hit the ball in the box one more time than your opponent and you win. That's the essence of it, but sometimes we make something more complicated out of it.

We get tied up in the surroundings; we get tied up with the adrenaline and excitement of it all. We get tied up in whether we should or shouldn't beat someone or think we should or shouldn't beat him, and it affects how we perform. It affects our focus on the match. Our expectations are sometimes too high or too low and our mind wanders. That's why the will to win is so important.

In college, we can coach while a match is going on. We cannot interrupt play, but I can talk to my players between serves and even between points. So if I see someone who is a little nervous, a little tight, I won't say, "Calm down," or, "You're too nervous; relax." I'll say, "Move your feet; get your racket back a little sooner," or, "Shrink the court. Give yourself five feet more within the sidelines."

I might ask him to keep the ball in play for ten hits and not to worry about whether he wins the point before his opponent. If it's 5-all and it's at a critical part of the third set and he starts to get tired a little bit, I'll say, "Serve this one into his body." In other words, I'll bring his focus back to the present, rather than to what might happen. I'll give him something to think about rather than letting him think about the result of what he might do. As I do that over and over again over the course of two or three years, it should start to sink in a little bit.

"Dick Gould, the tennis coach at Stanford, has the secret of the universe figured out and it is summed up in four words: *Make people feel important*. That's it right there. He succeeds fabulously."

—CHICO HAGEY,
all-American at Stanford,
NCAA tennis championship team

Chico Hagey

Winner of sixteen national tennis titles

The best athlete doesn't always win. Some people think they are supposed to win. I almost never lost a match I expected to win. I almost always lost when I expected to lose. The expression I use is *pre-loss*. This is a pre-loss match: I go through this huge, giant effort to convince my mind I can win, but if I think I'm supposed to lose, I lose.

When I was growing up, Raul Ramirez and I were doubles partners but we had never played top players. Then Raul took on ranked Bob Lutz in a singles match. I would have thought he would have been totally intimidated playing against a world-class player, yet he beat him 4 and 4. Some people don't have these same mind-wrestling matches as others and those people are the best players in the world. They're called winners.

"Every sport is about the fighting spirit, about winning as much as possible. You have to learn how to win and how to lose. Yes, you have to learn how to win, how not to become arrogant, because concealed within each victory is the seed for the next defeat if you make a mistake."

—HEINRICH VON PIERER,
CEO of Siemens AG and avid tennis player

Rod Laver

Only man to twice win all four Grand Slam
championships in the same year

There's so much to the game of tennis. It's mental to a large extent because confidence is such a very important part of being successful. Why do people play their best at Wimbledon or the U.S. Open? Pete Sampras plays his greatest tennis in the finals because that's when he has his best concentration. Certainly, knowledge of your opponent is a factor, as is being able to pull off the game that is needed to win the match. In the big tournaments around the world, tennis becomes a fairly extensive mental game.

When I played in my heyday, I would already know my opponent's game because I would have already played him a half a dozen times. I didn't really need a whole lot of preparation because it was plugged into my mind what this person preferred to do, how he played under pressure, if he'd crack, things that annoyed him, if the crowd or getting a bad call would upset him. All those things came into play, so I didn't have to go in with a set plan.

I might go in with the concept that if he had a very good return, I wouldn't serve and volley all the time. The little innuendos that came into play depended on how I was playing. If I was serving well, then I wouldn't care about his return. I would play my own game and let the match unfold on the court.

"You're never happy when you lose; you just want to keep winning. You always have to think positive."

—MARTINA HINGIS,
Wimbledon's youngest champion at age fifteen,
doubles with Helena Sukova

"It's unfair to say it was because of my arguing that people related to me. They sensed the passion, and they sensed I was somewhat frustrated by a very difficult game."

—JOHN MCENROE,
winner of seventeen Grand Slam titles

"When you go onto a tennis court, it's a fifty-fifty chance that you can win or you can lose. But I think the true champions have learned to see themselves only as winners."

—ZINA GARRISON,
Wimbledon finalist

Michael Chang

In 1989, at age seventeen, became the youngest ever French Open champion

When it comes to sports, the mind plays an incredible role. You're talking about perspectives, confidence, and attitude. All those characteristics play into what actually transpires on court.

I've always said you could have the most talented player, yet if he's not able to put it together in his mind, he won't win. If he goes up against a less talented player who mentally is tougher, more often than not the player who's mentally tougher will win.

A lot of it has to do with being able to put together all of your talents at the right time and in the right place. At the same time, your attitude and your perspective on court and how you see yourself and how much confidence you have in your game all contribute to what kind of tennis you can actually play on that day.

Mark McCormack

*Founder, chairman, and CEO of International
Management Group*

In tennis, when you're on the court in a match, you're hitting the ball 5 percent of the time, and 95 percent of the time you're either in changeovers or in between points. The flaw players have is they spend 99 percent of their time practicing the 5 percent and none of their time practicing the 95 percent. In other words, they should be practicing what to think about between points, what to think about on a changeover, what to look at, and what to be focusing on.

In many ways, I don't think tennis is as much of a mind game as golf is. I've often used the following analogy: Imagine what it would be like if you had an eight-foot putt on the 18th green to win the British Open. You take about five minutes to walk up to the green after your approach shot, contemplate those eight feet, watch your opponent putt out, and then you have to make your putt.

In tennis, this would be like having an overhead to win Wimbledon and the ball stayed in the air for five minutes. You'd now have time to think, "Okay, I have to keep my left arm extended, my right arm behind my back, stand in this position, the wind is from my left, be sure to keep my head up, and snap my wrists." That would make it a lot more difficult to hit that overhead.

Although there are elements that make tennis a mind game, there are a lot more elements that make it a reflex game. When you're at the net volleying, the ball's coming so fast, you don't have time to think about it. You do what your muscles and your training have taught you to do. Having said that, I think there are all kinds of examples where you get yourself psyched into winning or losing against an opponent.

It's harder when you're supposed to win than when you're not supposed to win. The player who's not supposed to win can just wing it, and if he loses, so what? The player who's supposed to win has the added pressure.

I once asked Bjorn Borg about what kind of draw he had at some tournament, and he said, "It doesn't make any difference. I'm number one in the world; I'm supposed to beat everybody, so it doesn't make any difference who I play."

"The key to being a champion is to peak yourself at the right time."

—MARK McCORMACK

"When I step on the court, I just worry about the ball."

—MONICA SELES,
*winner of the Australian Open, French Open,
and U.S. Open*

"I had to learn to like myself, to love my family. Now I enjoy playing, and it's showed up in the results."

—JENNIFER CAPRIATI,
*youngest pro finalist at
thirteen years, eleven months*

"The moment of victory is much too short to live for that and nothing else."

—MARTINA NAVRATILOVA,
winner of fifty-six Grand Slam titles

Tom Gullikson

1996 U.S. Olympic tennis coach

F irst of all, it's one-on-one combat. Tennis is not like golf, where it's just you and the ball and the course. Literally, you're playing against another person, and you don't have to play great, you just have to play better than that other person does on that particular day. It comes down to the will to win. If you have a lot of mental strength and self-belief, and you come on the court with a really good image of yourself, you can intimidate the opposing player.

One of the things we always stressed when we were working with players was that they compete well. A lot of the emphasis in teaching is placed on technique—having a good backhand, forehand, serve, and volley and under-standing technique—but a lot of our players are a little soft competitively.

That's one of the things my twin brother, Tim, taught Pete Sampras when he started working with him. He taught Pete how to compete and win. He showed him how to use his athletic ability on the days that he wasn't striking the ball particularly well. That's an art and a skill and it's some-thing you can work on, but you have to be willing to put on your blue collar and go to work when you're out on the court.

"Being number one is almost a passion. It's something that you're consumed with. For years, I just wanted to win majors and to finish the year number one. That was always my goal."

—PETE SAMPRAS,
winner of a record thirteen
Grand Slam singles titles

"The major tournaments are what's going to keep me in the game for a lot of years. I put so much pressure on myself to do well at the majors that it makes all the hard work I put into the game worhwhile."

—PETE SAMPRAS

"When I feel like I can't contend for the majors, when I feel like I am playing just to play or that I'm not enjoying it, that will be my time."

—PETE SAMPRAS

Dennis Ralston

Director of tennis at the Broadmore Hotel,
Colorado Springs, Colorado

To be good, you have to be able to control the mental part of the frustrations that occur when you miss. You also have to be competitive, which is a mind factor. I don't know anybody who's very good who doesn't like to compete. You can have the best shots in the game and not be mentally into it, meaning you're not competitive, and you won't win.

I think it's like any sport, from chess to fly-fishing. When I first started to fly-fish, it was very frustrating. I would hook myself and hook myself, but as I got better, I realized my mental frame of reference was that it was a challenge. It's a mental game trying to fool those fish.

Tennis is more than hitting the ball; it's being able to handle the bad calls, bad bounces, bad breaks, and not let them fluster you. It's a phase of the game that's so very important, yet no one has the key. No one I've met, including the sports psychologists, knows the answer. They will give their ideas, but they don't often work. That's why they bounce around and everybody's still trying to find the key. Any attempt, like this book, that can help people understand it better should be a big seller.

Pam Shriver

Ranked in the top ten in the world nine times,
1980–1988

In singles, you're out there all alone; there's no legal coaching during competition. It's a very lonely place to be and when it's lonely, the mind can do some incredible things, both good and bad. When you know it's only you, if you're at all vulnerable, you can get very uneasy. You can get very anxious and nervous about situations that maybe a month later when you have your game together you wouldn't even bat an eyelash.

The difference between feeling confident on the singles court and feeling vulnerable and a bit shaky is unbelievable, as is the difference between doing something you know you do well and wondering whether or not you can complete the assignment. You have all these doubts, it's like you're not the same person. Very little time can pass between one extreme and the other. I really think it's because you are alone.

"Once you understand your fears, your emotions, it's easier to conquer them."

—PAM SHRIVER

Chris Evert

Thirteen-time Wightman Cup team member,
singles record 26–0

The mental part of the game is the deciding factor, but some players never got it. They were brilliantly talented players, but they never understood. This is where Martina Navratilova improved. She started out with all the physical ability in the world, and then she really worked on her mental game.

I don't think she ever matched my mental level because she was so good physically. She'd win three points just because of her athleticism. But she got to that next level mentally and it paid off, because then she dominated.

"Great athletes are defined as much as anything by having great competitors, great competition."

—CHRIS EVERT

"There were times when deep down inside I wanted to win so badly I could actually will it to happen."

—CHRIS EVERT

"There are role models all around. Chris Evert, an unknown sixteen-year-old, got to the semifinals of the U.S. Open. It was the first time I realized a girl could be great. It changed my entire perspective. I thought, 'Well, wait a minute, maybe I can be a professional athlete.' Chris Evert changed my whole life."

—MARY CARILLO,
television commentator and
former professional tennis player

Teresa Edwards

Record five-time member of the U.S. Olympic women's basketball team

Tennis is different from basketball in that it's an individual sport, but it's the same in that you still have to prepare your mind to compete at your best. Before a basketball game, I focus on what I have to do individually at the offensive end of the floor and then I shift to what I have to do in my position defensively. I size up my competition. There's a lot of mental preparation every step of the way.

The mind-set is powerful before you step onto the tennis court. In my mind, I'm a great tennis player before I get out there. When I put the tennis racket in my hand, it feels really good. But as soon as the ball bounces toward me, the truth comes out and I know the difference between being a basketball player and a tennis player. In basketball, I'm trying to dictate and destroy; in tennis, I'm trying to survive.

George Dunklin

Nine-time Arkansas State tennis champion

Tennis is a mind game because it's an individual sport. It's you against the other guy. There are different tactics and different strokes for every match. The really good players read their opponents and figure out the kind of game that they have to play against them.

Just to go out and play straight tennis and hit your shots may be all right for club players, but when you get to the tournament level, the mind really comes into it. All of the top players can hit the ball. They all can serve at 130 mph. There's not a great deal of difference in the caliber of the strokes between any of them. It gets down to the will to win.

Passion is the driving force of champions. I have a little book by Jimmy Connors in which he said that with every stroke he made, he was trying to figure that stroke in reference to where he was going to hit the next one. It wasn't just a question of sitting there and hitting the ball.

You never hear much about the mind in tennis, but it is very, very important. It is the diference between being average and being great.

"I really love to play. I can't say it enough. I really enjoy the game. When I was a little kid, I could go on and on playing against a wall. I think every person has a passion in life, and mine is for tennis."

—MONICA SELES,
first major title, French Open, 1990

"I hate to lose more than I like to win. I hate to see the happiness on their faces when they beat me!"

—JIMMY CONNORS,
International Tennis Hall of Fame

"I always play with a bunch of emotion. It's just part of my game. I just go with my instinct. I like to get fans into the match, because I love an intense atmosphere."

—ANDY RODDICK,
rising U.S. tennis star

Robert Conrad

Star of the television miniseries
James Michener's Centennial

The first thing I like about tennis is, if you play against someone of an equal level, you have to outsmart him. You have to put the ball where he isn't, and that takes a certain skill. It also takes anticipation. The brain wins the game.

By analyzing the other player, I know if a guy has a shot he's soft on. I know that if I play him deep on his backhand, he's going to give me a floater. I can move to the net. He knows that when he plays against me, I have my short strokes. I like to run to the ball. When I run to the ball, he makes a great lob. I call it the sky ball. If anyone reads your book in my tennis cluster, I'm done. They like to beat me, but I'm competitive.

"Where's the Viagra? I've got to get up!"

—ROBERT CONRAD

"I don't mind losing. What I mind is not performing to my level."

—ROBERT CONRAD

CHAPTER THREE

Head Games

"If I don't do what I need to do to win, I won't win, no matter who's on the other side of the net."

—ANDRE AGASSI,
first unseeded man to win the U.S. Open

Bill Bond

U.S. Professional Tennis Association (USPTA)
Master Professional

The head game is really very important, but you have to solve the hitting, the playing of the ball first. All the positive thinking in the world won't help unless you've paid the price on the practice court. You've got to have that as your foundation. You can carry it beyond that with hard physical-fitness work, more now than before. They work hand in hand. One breeds the other.

For instance, Jennifer Capriati really turned the corner when she broke up with her boyfriend, got a little more serious, and started training harder. Everybody noticed she had lost some weight. All of a sudden, she was moving better and hitting the ball harder. Then, of course, her mental game improved because she thought, "Hey, I'm a better player now and I'm capable." Suddenly she wins the Australian and she's at a different level.

Jennifer knows she's up to the task. Whereas if you're not really able to fight hard for a long period of time and you're not strong enough to dive for balls and you don't have quite the strength to drive through the ball for two, three, four hours, people are going to beat you.

It has a little to do with mental toughness, but you have to pay the price; you have to have the foundation. I think a lot of the players, even professionals, keep playing when they shouldn't. They should take some time off. If you get a little stale competing, you end up losing your confidence and you might not ever be able to reconstruct it.

"Before, I didn't do the right things and didn't expect to win. But now I am doing everything I should and I believe I deserve to win."

—JENNIFER CAPRIATI,
Australian and French Open champion

"I played with no fear when I was younger because I had no expectations and no pressure. That's how I feel now. I've been playing well because no one has really expected much of me at all. I always felt somehow that I would find my way back. I knew that I would come back despite all the bad stuff that went down. I'm no longer going to doubt myself. Now I know anything is possible."

—JENNIFER CAPRIATI

Charlie Pasarell

Lost to Pancho Gonzales in the longest
match in Wimbledon history (1969),
22–24, 1–6, 16–14, 6–3, 11–9 (112 games)

Tennis is certainly a sport that requires tremendous athletic ability. You have to be fast, have quick reactions, a good touch, very good eyesight, and a sense of anticipation, a knowledge of where things are going to happen. Players like John McEnroe and Rod Laver were born with those gifts. Other people don't have the same level of gifts that they had. They have to work harder to try to develop these abilities.

Tennis is also a game where you are out there by yourself. It's not somebody passing or handing a ball to you or blocking for you or setting up a screen. You're all by yourself. You basically have to execute by yourself. You don't have anybody else helping you in this process. So, you have to get yourself in an extremely good frame of mind to be able to handle all this by yourself.

Everybody gets nervous. I don't care who you are. You get the sweaty palms. Your breathing changes. Pancho Gonzales once said, "To be able to *use* that nervousness and *channel* that nervousness in a positive way, to make yourself stronger and faster, to make yourself think clearer, is really something you have to work at."

Some people handle it very well and some people don't. That's usually when people choke. They don't handle the critical moment in the match very well. Beyond that, tennis is sort of a chess game. The other sport I can compare tennis to is boxing. You really have to see, to look for openings, whether it's attacking someone's backhand or changing the pace.

Some players play very well if you give them pace. However, if you vary the pace, you can throw them off. It's similar to a pitcher throwing to a batter. Some guys can handle the fastball all the time. If you give them change-ups and curveballs and move the ball around, you can exploit their weaknesses.

It's not only about you making winners. In fact, it is less about making winning shots than about playing a shot that can actually force your opponent to make an error. Even at the pro level, close to 75 percent of all the points won are on an opponent's missed shot rather than a winning shot.

Tennis is a game that requires tremendous willpower. You need to have a great mind when you reach a critical point in a match, the moment of truth, because you have to be able to handle it. All of a sudden, it's in your hand, it's on your racket. How do you respond? You don't feel the same. Your feet don't feel like they're quite on the ground. Your breathing is changing. You're wondering how to overcome all that. How do you take that nervous energy and channel it so that you can think clearly? It's a game that requires a tremendous amount of thought and preparation.

I learned from the great Pancho Gonzales. The best advice he ever gave to me was that you have to prepare long before the match. When I was attending UCLA, I used to ask Pancho all kinds of questions about how he did this, how he did that, and how did such-and-such a player play. One time I said, "Pancho, if you have to play a big match, how do you prepare yourself for it?" He said, "Every match that you play is a big match. When you stop thinking it's a big match, that's the match you are going to lose. When you get out there, it's the most important match you're ever going to play."

Another piece of advice was how to prepare. Pancho told me, "I like to go and try to find a quiet place in the locker room or somewhere where I can just sit down, close my eyes, and spend ten to fifteen minutes visualizing what I'm going to do. Most of the time, you know your opponents and how they play. You know what they do best and what they like to do. It's not so much about analyzing what I need to do against my opponent, it's trying to analyze what I'm going to do in this particular match at the critical times. I begin by visualizing the warm-up. I try to visualize hitting the ball and moving up to the net and making some volleys and how I'm going to execute my volleys. Also, I visualize how I'm going to warm up my serve.

"Then I visualize whether I'll choose to serve or receive if I win the toss of the coin. I make that decision ahead of time so when the toss of the coin happens, my decision will have already been made. Then I think about how I'm going to play the first game. If it's my serve, I'm going to play it this way. If I'm receiving, I imagine what kind of returns I'm going to make. Then I consider how I'm going to play the first break point. And if I'm serving for the first set, how I'm going to serve."

Pancho visualized all those circumstances and how he was going to be playing each one. The reason he did that was because when you're out there and all of a sudden you're under pressure and you're nervous, it's hard to have a clear mind as to what you're going to do. So you have to have rehearsed it. You don't want to ad-lib on the court. At least in your mind, you're warmed up. You're ready. You already know what to do when you face those kinds of situations.

It's one thing to warm up physically and then it's another thing to face the first break point. You start thinking, "What do I do? Do I chip this return or do I go for it? Do I run around to my backhand? Or do I try to hit a backhand?" What you want to do is to have made that decision a half an hour before the match.

Pancho used to tell me it was difficult for him at tournaments like Wimbledon to find a quiet place, so he used to lock himself in the toilet, the W.C. He said he didn't need to go to the bathroom, but he'd go in there for ten to fifteen minutes because it was the only place he could close his eyes and visualize what he was going to be doing on the court.

Tennis is a game that requires a lot of strategy. It is also a game in which you must know a lot about yourself, your own state of mind, and how you control the emotions you're going to experience in a match.

"The worst thing that can happen to any athlete, performer, entertainer, actor, is to get nervous and not know what to do. You have to know what to do. If you know what you're going to do, if you know how you'll execute, you're going to be just fine."

—CHARLIE PASARELL

"If your opponent starts throwing a temper tantrum, be prepared. Be ready for it. Know how to act. Don't get involved in it. Don't let it upset you."

—CHARLIE PASARELL

Nick Bollettieri

Renowned tennis coach, Bollettieri Tennis Academy,
Bradenton, Florida

In singles, you're out there one-on-one. You're not involved with anyone else. When it's one-on-one, you can't hide; everything comes out. Whether you're folding or you put up when the time is right, it shows a lot of your features. It clearly will show the type of person you are when it gets down to the final push-and-shove. Certain things come out.

The great players find a way to win. If you look at Monica Seles or Andre Agassi or Pete Sampras, all the greats, when they're down and out, they somehow find a way to come through. The reason why is because you have to beat a champion; you can't wait for them to lose.

I use a little barometer. Early on when teaching boys and girls, the majority of emphasis is placed on techniques, foundations, stances, hands, and grips. That's 80 percent of the game. When that starts to take hold and the players fall into their individual styles of play with good foundations, the mental parts begin to take over and the barometer begins to change.

The barometer can go as high 80 percent mental and 20 percent technique. But as Tiger Woods has said, "You can't let the techniques go, because little things seem to creep up." That's the danger point, because if you don't tend to the little things, they will amount to a big thing.

"I'm not a big stat guy. I'm trying to focus on what I need to do. Stats are good to hear about, but they really don't help me put the ball in the court. I'm not motivated by stats."

—ANDY RODDICK,
at nineteen, the youngest player in the 2001 Association of Tennis Professionals' (ATP's) top twenty

"I love competition. I like the individuality of tennis. You have to rely on yourself, and that makes things interesting."

—ANDY RODDICK

"I really don't have any long-term goals. I don't say I want to be number one in the world. I just want to keep improving. Every three or four months for the last year and a half, I've stepped it up a level. I think if I can continue to do that, things should take care of themselves."

—ANDY RODDICK

Todd Martin

All-American at Northwestern, and top-ranked
NCAA tennis player, 1989–1990

What challenges your mental capacity is when you get to a certain level of proficiency technically and then competition challenges you to be able to execute those techniques throughout different emotional states.

I think if you were to put the top thirty players on a tennis court and just have them hit shots, you'd be impressed with every one of them. This is not to say they're all of equal capabilities, but it's close enough to think that any one of them could win against any other any day. It doesn't necessarily happen because the best players are able to sum up the ability to execute when nobody else can, when it's the most difficult situation presented.

Most of the times when I've come back from being down two sets to love have been against players who, when I walked out on the court, I was thinking I was better than they were. I didn't necessarily expect to win, but I expected a chance to win. Being down two sets to love right away is not the way I envisioned the matches going. Then I tried to figure out if there was something strategically I could do differently. That should be one of the only cognitive responses to it all, "I must do something different." I tinker with that a little bit.

I honestly believe the roles become reversed in a situation where the guy who walked out on the court thinking he had nothing to lose is suddenly playing better than his opponent. All of a sudden he has something to lose. He probably has a 90 percent chance to win the match and then, of course, his opponent's role is reversed as well. Having that feeling of nothing to lose is very encouraging and frees the body to execute the way you know you can. Essentially your mind leaves the result out of it. All of a sudden, it's, "I need to do better than what I'm doing; let's see if I can do that."

"There comes a time when you just have to stop caving. In the end, I told myself, 'You're going to have to perform.' And that's what I did."

—SERENA WILLIAMS,
upon winning the 1999 U.S. Open

"It's like love. When you look too hard, you don't find it. When you let it happen naturally, it comes."

—MARAT SAFIN,
*2000 U.S. Open champion
talking about finding his game*

Ahmad Rashad

Host of NBA television show Inside Stuff

When you start playing tennis, it's just run and fetch until you can play well enough that it becomes a mind game. It's not mental when you first start playing. It's all physical. It's all run, get to the ball, knock it back over the net. Once you master that, it's run, get to the ball, and knock it to a place over the net. And then it's run, get to the ball, and knock it to a place where the other guy can only return it to a particular place. Now you're playing tennis.

Everybody who plays tennis doesn't play tennis. Eventually, you get to the point where you are playing a mental game. It's not just hitting the ball around. Each time you hit the ball, you're setting up for a return to come to the place where you think it's going to come, and that's why great players don't run very much.

I used to play with John McEnroe in my ultimate tennis years. John and I would play all the time. I always ran. John never ran. He'd always be standing, set up, with his racket back ready to hit the ball. Me, I'd be scrambling with all my agility and speed, and he'd say to me, "God, you're fast." I wanted to say, "Let me see how fast you are." But I could never make him run.

It's the mental part that makes tennis so much fun. You start working points. There's no more beauty than to watch a point being set up to the end. You hit it to his backhand, then you hit it to his forehand; you hit it short, then cross-court. You come in, and you put it away.

"Bad shots are temporary. They happen to everybody. You realize it's all about the next one; it's not about the one you just hit. It's not about the shot you just missed. It's always about the next shot. Not only in sports, but in life, too, it's always about the next one."

—AHMAD RASHAD

"Everybody loves success, but they hate successful people."

—JOHN MCENROE,
*NCAA tennis champion as a Stanford freshman,
and three-time Wimbledon champion*

"In the past, I always thought I could do it. I was young. I was cocky. I thought the best was ahead of me. I didn't have the self-doubts I did this time around. Now I'm really enjoying it. And I need that. I need to enjoy something that has been so good to me over the years."

—ANDRE AGASSI,
ranked number one in the world in 1999

"I give every player so much respect on the court, as far as their game goes, because that's the way I perform my best."

—ANDRE AGASSI

"I feel old when I see mousse in my opponent's hair."

—ANDRE AGASSI

Scott Bondurant

National junior doubles champion and
former captain of the Stanford tennis team

Junior tennis puts a lot of pressure on kids in terms of playing an individual sport as opposed to a team sport, because you're out there very much on your own. You have to figure it out by yourself. That alone makes it a difficult mind game.

As a junior player, you get into a pecking order where you feel like you should beat certain kids and certain other kids should beat you. There's an enormous fear of losing to somebody you shouldn't lose to.

The flip side of that is it's a big hurdle if you're not supposed to beat a certain player. Trying to figure out a way to get over that is hard. You don't think you should, so you don't. It's easy to assume you'll lose.

Somehow in a one-on-one sport like tennis, it's remarkable how you figure out where you belong in the pecking order, and making big changes in that pecking order is tough. It's an evolution, but you end up finding your place.

Billy Martin

UCLA tennis coach

I see a lot of head games at the college level. There's a pecking order for the players that remains from when they were younger. They are still losing to the same players they did when they were twelve and thirteen. That almost gets to be a mind frame. Trying to overcome that is sometimes very difficult. To really believe that you're better than the guy who was a year or two older than you, whom you always looked up to, can be a mental hurdle.

This is true at the college level and a little bit at the pro level. I remember back in my day looking at Arthur Ashe and John Newcombe and all of a sudden, seven years down the line, I'm playing against them and thinking, "Oh, God, can I beat my idols?"

Most players get really tentative and tight when it comes to closing it out. I keep preaching to my players that there are so many great front runners, so many great first-set players, but what counts is if they can close it out when they get to midpoint in the second set, when they can begin to see the finish line. So many players really start to drop their level at that particular time. On the other hand, great players, when it comes time to close it out, really raise their level.

I have players who really try to win. They work so hard and they play great in practice. Then all of a sudden it comes match time and their level drops off. I think they put too much internal pressure on themselves. There are other players who drive a coach nutty because they're so lackadaisical, so happy-go-lucky, during practice. But when they get in a match, they don't seem to tighten up, they stay relaxed. They're a constant the whole way. From a coaching standpoint, I've had to change my ideas a little bit about the players who are a little looser in practice.

Everybody sees himself drifting a little bit mentally; it's how fast you regain your balance that counts. How forgiving mentally are you to yourself? Are you going to be your worst critic or are you going to be your biggest supporter and helper?

Most of the top pros will play a bad point, but the next point, they're right back in it, whereas the players who are weaker mentally go a game or two before they get it back, and sometimes they're so discouraged with themselves that they never get it back. I think you have to be a little bit realistic and see what's happening. Focus right away, be determined to play a great point that next point whether you win it or lose it, and take it for what it is.

It's a mental game in that you really don't find out what strokes break down in tennis until you get to crucial times, crucial points. The first point of a game is no indication to me whether or not the strokes are going to hold up or break down. It's the break points; it's the big deuce points; it's when you're serving in the tiebreaker. That's when I really love watching players and really finding out what's holding up and what's breaking down, stroke-wise and mental-wise.

It takes the competitive matches where it's really on the line to figure out where your players are at and if they're improving. This goes not only for strokes and choking, but for temperament. A lot of players suddenly blow up at the least little thing when the pressure's on, and to me, that's just sort of masking the whole thing. That's like waving a flag that they're starting to get nervous. They're trying to find excuses why they're not going to win.

"There are three realms in tennis. There's the emotional game, which is between points. There's the mental game, which is during the point. And there's the physical game, which encompasses strokes and physical conditioning."

—JEFF MOORE,
University of Texas women's tennis coach

Lornie Kuhle

Tennis director, MGM Grand Hotel, Las Vegas

The thing that Jimmy Connors and Bobby Riggs both shared in common was that they didn't really play their opponent. What they did was play the tennis ball and worry about how they were hitting the ball. It didn't matter who was on the other side of the net. They were trying to figure out how they were striking the ball. They focused on how they were playing and not on how the other person was playing. Not many people can get to that level of tennis.

I traveled with Jimmy for ten years. He never looked at the draw sheets. When he played tournaments, he just went out and played his opponent and found out the next day who his next opponent was. One time, we were in Vermont playing a tournament and we went into the little trailer before the finals and there was a guy in there; I believe his name was Mike Cahill. Jimmy looked at him and said, "How did you do in the tournament, Mike?" And Mike said, "Well, I'm playing you in the finals." And Jimmy said, "Oh, really?" Jimmy truly didn't know. Talk about psychological play.

That was it for Cahill right there. Jimmy beat him love and 1 in the finals. It was for real. Jimmy had no idea who he was playing because he didn't read the newspapers, he didn't look at the draw, it didn't make any difference. He'd win his match, leave the court, and get away from everything. That guy in Vermont had no chance in the first place and after what happened in the trailer, he *really* had no chance.

"Most sports are mind games. When you think of the champions in tennis, you see very tough-minded people."

—Raquel Gisafre,
former professional tour player and
cofounder of Promotion Sports

Donald Dell

Chairman of ProServ and six-time
member of the U.S. Davis Cup team

Tennis is not as much of a head game as golf. For me, golf is much more mental than physical. Tennis is more physical than mental, and the mental part of the game you learn almost by habit or instinct. You play it so much that you react a certain way. If I hit a first serve and come in and make a volley, I'm not thinking about it; I just do it by habit.

Tennis is more determined by who you're playing and how he plays than is golf, where you're really playing yourself. In tennis, you're playing somebody, and how he plays affects everything you do. Mostly it's reflective reactions based on habit.

For example, when I go out and play golf, I have to think about every stroke and what I'm going to do, how to address the ball that's just sitting there. If I go to play tennis and I play for an hour, I can hit the ball as well as I ever did; I just don't run as well or I don't serve as hard, but my strokes all come back. I know the speed of the ball, I know the grips, because I've done it for so long.

Tennis is much more physical if you're comparing it to golf. If you're not, tennis can become very mental. You're out there in an individual sport, you're serving a second serve, it's 30–40 in the fifth set, and there's a chance to choke or to miss a serve or to miss a volley. There's a lot of time to think if you're rallying from the baseline.

There's also a lot of time if you're playing on red clay or a slow surface like the French Open. Matches are four hours long; that's mental and physical because you get tired and you have plenty of time on the rallies to think about if you'll hit a topspin or if you're going to slice it or you're going to go for the drop shot.

"The mind does unbelievable things."

—NICK BOLLETTIERI,
outstanding tennis coach

"You've got to be mentally tough as well as have good strokes."

—DODO CHENEY,
winner of more than 300 national tennis titles

"Tennis is a sport of momentum."

—MARAT SAFIN,
2000 U.S. Open champion

Pam Shriver

*Won a record twenty major doubles championships
with partner Martina Navratilova*

When Martina Navratilova called me in October of 1980 to be her doubles partner, it was the defining moment of my career. I needed to step up. I needed to play well and handle the pressure of playing with one of the great, if not the greatest, female tennis player of all times.

Some people said that would be easy because she was so good. That's not the way it works. You really feel the pressure to hold up your own end and to do your share of the work. Our doubles developed quite naturally and easily for us. We lost our first tournament to the then number one team in the world. But we won our second tournament and we won the first major we played together, Wimbledon 1981. By the second year, we were really locked in. We had a string of two and a half years where we never lost a match and had 109 consecutive victories. Obviously, when you win, you enjoy yourself, and we clicked really nicely.

In doubles, because there's another person with you, there are twice as many things that can go right and twice as many things that can go wrong. There are all kinds of communication strategies you can use in doubles to help settle things down, whether it's tactical or just psychological. Talking, laughing, pointing out little trends that the opponents are doing, are some examples. You can achieve so many things by talking.

For instance, if you know your partner is going to serve a big serve out wide, and your opponents are going to be struggling to reach to get it, that is no time to make an intercept; you have to guard your line. You have to communicate these things with a quick word. Usually it's just, "Out wide and go." *Out wide and go* means serve out wide and you poach, you intercept.

That's a dangerous one, but if you've at least set it up, the server has a chance to get over. Usually it would be up-the-middle-and-look-for-it. Up-the-middle-and-look-for-it isn't a full poach; it's like up the middle and you'd better be leaning because my serve's going to be good enough that the return is probably going to be a floater somewhere that you can get.

Other times, doubles strategy warrants more of a discussion, and sometimes it can be very complicated because the opponents are doing things that are really upsetting to your rhythm. One of your opponents could be on a roll with her return. Or, it could be that it's been a long game and you have to figure out what to do now to try and confuse the returner. You could change the pace, go in a different direction, use the "I" formation or the Australian formation, or you could stay regular and do a big fake like you're poaching. When it gets complicated, there are a lot of different choices, and it's a lot of fun.

Betsy Nagelson

Won twenty-five doubles titles worldwide, including two Australian Opens

E very sport is really a head game. But tennis certainly is a one-only. You're out there on your own. You're competing against another person, so there are a lot of elements wrapped up in that. The good news about tennis is it's very physical, so you get to concentrate on a lot more elements than just those on the mental side.

The reality is that this sport is mostly mental because the actual time you're spending hitting a tennis ball is not very much compared to the time that you're walking between points or changing sides. Tennis certainly gives you a lot of time to devote to the mental side, but you have to be ready to make very quick decisions, and that also makes it a difficult mental game.

Playing on grass when it's really fast makes it even more of a head game. You're more mentally exhausted when you're finished. You realize it's quicker, so you don't have as much time to make your decisions and choices, so the ones you make are more critical. We're talking sport here, not life, but it seems the consequences are greater if you don't make a right decision. You can get away with some poor choices on a slower court because it's hard to put the ball away. You can neutralize a point pretty quickly, but on a faster surface you can't.

Mary Carillo

Outspoken television tennis commentator

I was so lucky that Billie Jean King became a very good friend of mine early on and I was able to play team tennis with her and practice with her. I always felt that sitting next to Billie Jean as she was barking to herself on a changeover, listening to her vent, taught me some of the greatest tennis lessons of my life. It was fascinating to see how her mind worked.

Inside her head there was a civil war going on. She would have just lost her serve and she'd come over on the changeover, and say, "Na-na-na-na, I can't believe your toss, na-na-na-na." By the end of it, she'd have made up with herself. She'd be saying, "Now, come on, one point at a time. Get in the moment; stay in the moment."

She could collect herself and figure out what the hell she was doing. She was so smart and she had such a good sense of what was happening on the other side of the court.

Sometimes she switched over and asked herself, "Why am I getting tight? That chick on the other side is having conniptions." That's when she knew to lengthen the points, lengthen the rallies, because her opponent was tighter.

"People don't feel safe with people who stretch them."

—BILLIE JEAN KING,
International Tennis Hall of Fame

"Whatever you fear, go there."

—BILLIE JEAN KING

"I felt lonely a lot. It wasn't easy being out front."

—BILLIE JEAN KING

Alan Thicke

Star of the television series Growing Pains

The most amazing athletes in the world to me are the tennis players who can play at the level they do for over three hours. There's nothing that I enjoy for three hours. I think I've had some fun in my life, but I don't know that there's anything in my life I can stay enthused about for three hours.

I have a low attention span, which might be why I've been divorced twice. The level of concentration and physicality required in tennis makes it one of the most remarkable of all sports. I endorse the Alan Thicke method of perpetual mediocrity: Do not take lessons, do not stretch, do not buy one of those ball machines, and do not hit the ball against the wall a million times.

CHAPTER FOUR

Focus

*"It's really hard to be
100 percent focused
and 100 percent relaxed
because they don't go
hand in hand."*

—STAN SMITH,
supplied the clinching third point for victory,
in Davis Cup play a record six times

Ted Schroeder
International Tennis Hall of Fame

When you start to lose your focus in a match, you immediately go to your mental checklist of four or five things. It doesn't take long before the bell goes off. As you're walking between points or changing sides, you decide on your next move.

For instance, if all of a sudden I'm having trouble with my serve, I ask myself, "Where am I tossing the ball?" I know where I have to toss it. Maybe my concentration is wandering and I'm not tossing the ball right. Another time, I may be hitting too many forehands in the net instead of hitting through the ball. So I tell myself I might be starting low and lifting too high, too fast, which causes a miss-hit and the ball goes in the net.

Everybody knows how everybody else serves. If you start missing a lot of returns or you can't get to a lot of returns, you check what your position is on the court. This changes on the first serve as opposed to the second serve. Then you try to think, "What's this guy doing? He was serving wide to my forehand in the deuce court, which opened up the one down the middle. Is he still doing that? If he is, is my play correct? I should move in so I can protect both shots and not get drawn out of the court if he serves the wide one."

On the volleys, there are two fundamentals: You have to keep the racket head above your wrist at all times and you have to keep the ball in front of you at all times. When you play a ground stroke, you play the ball from the midposition of your body. You make your contact at that point. On the volley, you're way out in front. If you start missing volleys, you check where you're hitting that ball. Everybody has his own little checklist.

"You see players like Jimmy Connors and Bjorn Borg, and you couldn't interrupt their thought processes ever. Once they got on the court for practice or to play, they were completely focused."

—JOHN STEEL,
two-time Ivy League champion

"I once said to Bjorn Borg, 'Okay, you're serving in a match that means nothing and you are now serving match point to win Wimbledon. What do you think about differently?' He said, 'You try to take the occasion out of the point and just focus on the mechanics.'"

—MARK McCORMACK,
best-selling author of What They Don't Teach You at Harvard Business School

Michael Chang

Tennis Magazine's *Male Rookie of the Year, 1988*

The first thing you do when you lose focus is to concentrate on what's going right. When you concentrate on what's going wrong, everything else starts to affect it, beginning a chain reaction. I think the perspective and attitude that you take is very important.

A lot of times I can see a match turn by a point here or a point there. Players have an opportunity and they're not able to take advantage of it, or they miss a bad shot and get so frustrated that it affects subsequent points. Points become games and games become sets. Pretty soon, before you know it, the match is over and you've lost.

Your perspective and attitude play a very important role. Sometimes you're playing very bad and yet you have a positive perspective that things will turn around. You say, "Let's work at it; I can do it." And things start to change in your game. You see your opponent getting frustrated and the whole tide of the match turns.

"My personality has never been one that I go out just to play the game of tennis and enjoy myself. I'm the type of person who when I go into something, I give it my all; otherwise, I don't go into it at all. I love to compete, to be out there playing the tough matches."

—MICHAEL CHANG

"You not only have to play physically, but you have to play mentally. The brighter students who are equally athletic are the ones who win. It doesn't take any practice to play dumb. It's the smarter ones who find a way to win."

—BEN PRESS,
U.S. Professional Tennis Association (USPTA)
Master Professional and winner of
thirteen national titles

"As you begin to tire, as a match wears on, you have a tendency to get dumber. If you can, in concert as you start to fatigue, try to concentrate harder."

—BEN PRESS

Tom Gullikson

1996 U.S. Olympic tennis coach

When you start to lose your focus, you have to kick yourself and say, "Now, in tennis, dummy, I can only play one point at a time. So let's get some present focus going here." There are only two things you do in tennis: You're either serving the ball or you're returning the ball. If you're serving, you need to take your time and visualize where you're serving. Literally picture the type of serve you want to hit going to a certain place in the box and really focus in on just serving.

If you're returning on the men's tour, you basically have to dial 911 because most guys are serving the ball 125 or 130 mph on the first serve. On the first serve, you're just trying to survive and get the ball back, and on the second serve, you're planning what you're going to do.

If my opponent serves to my forehand, I'm going to do this. If he serves to my backhand, I'm going to do that. You try to really get involved in the process, lose yourself, and focus on the moment. Then you can let the winning and losing take care of itself.

Betsy Nagelson

Three-time U.S. Open senior women's doubles champion

I'm convinced that when you're doing a physical activity, your mind is in a heightened state and you think clearer. You make some of your best decisions when you're in a physical mood and your heart rate is up. I actually believe this could be proven scientifically. I know that if I need to pack for a trip, I'll go hit balls and I'll do a perfect pack job.

When you're playing tennis for your livelihood and you're in the semi-finals of some big tournament, I'm not terribly convinced that it's a horrible thing to think about things unrelated to tennis such as what you're going to have for dinner. It's a whole lot more positive than thinking negative thoughts such as, "I wish my forehand was better," or, "Don't hit it to her backhand."

It's often possible to get yourself into a panic mode, but if you're thinking, "Yeah, I'm going to have veal tonight," you're in a more positive state. That's not necessarily optimal to your top performance, though. A lot of what is required is discipline in all areas of your mind.

Instead of just saying, "I panic at the end and can't close a match or a set out," you need to say, "Okay, when I get to that point, I'll have a strategy and accept the fact that in the past, I haven't done a great job." Then you look forward to being in that position again and figuring another way to improve. If I had it to do all over again, I would have approached the whole mental side of tennis that way, as opposed to feeling like a louse for not being able to concentrate for a whole match.

Another big problem today for young and old athletes is spending too much time comparing yourself to the superstar in your field and wondering why you can't perform like they do. Tiger Woods is so great that every golfer now just isn't going to measure up. This may or may not be true, but that's not the relevant part. Tiger still wins and loses golf tournaments and so can any other golfer. It's really easy to get into a place where you compare yourself and then you have a hard time separating the mental from the physical.

It's like when you put music on. If you watch a player play with music on, they automatically play better. It's not that they're concentrating on their tennis. It's just that they get into that zone where they're going to the rhythm of the music and they're less negative in their mind. They're focused. It's difficult to explain why, but they're out there loving it, having a good time, hitting the ball great and enjoying themselves.

"When you're playing really well, you're not really thinking about anything; it's all just sort of happening. The thought process seems to come in when you're starting to play bad. And then you start thinking about things and that usually screws you up more."

—MONICA SELES,
winner of nine Grand Slam championships

"The only ball that counts is the one that's coming at you."

—BILLIE JEAN KING,
tennis legend

"Usually when you're playing well, you're a bit on automatic pilot. You're certainly not thinking about technique and hopefully you're not thinking about the situation."

—STAN SMITH,
U.S. Open and Wimbledon champion

Sally Huss
Wimbledon semifinalist and acclaimed artist

There are so many avenues to divert focus, but when the energy is there and you're totally relaxed, you're in tune with the whole of what's going on. You're much more apt to be at the right place at the right time and be in tune with the ball.

If you're focused too much on wanting to win, you're not in harmony with the whole of what's going on. I think that's the key. You need to be very open when you play and not too wanting, because your system already knows you're attempting to win. By not demanding too much of yourself, you'll find it is far easier to focus and tennis becomes much more enjoyable.

This also applies to my painting and to life. If you're more open to what the brush will do, what the paint will do, what the atmosphere will do at that time, rather than demanding a preconceived idea of perfection, what happens is always a result of everything. So, to be a part of everything is better than being terribly willful and trying to force that upon what you're doing. My art is very free and light-hearted and the colors are bright. That's the way I paint and the way I now play tennis.

I played tennis two ways. First I played traditional tennis, before there was any money or professional tennis. I went through the same kind of thinking that most people do, which is fearful. There was a great deal of fear—what happens if I lose this point, what happens if I lose this set? There were always demands made on the shot that I was winding up to hit.

The second way I played tennis was after I had done a lot of Zen work and freed up my motion and spirit. Once I saw that I performed a lot better when I was relaxed and freer and more spontaneous, tennis became much more exciting. I had a lot of power and enthusiasm for what I was doing. I played much better, but I was much, much older by then, so I was out of the loop as far as being a money winner. I was in the top twenty when I was thirty-four, but I just played for the fun of it.

When you don't care whether you win or lose, you play full out. Then you're really dangerous because you can win. If you don't care about the outcome and you're just playing for that point right there, that ball right there, then you possess a lot more power. You are more dangerous because your energies are not conflicted. You're not demanding something back.

Most people go out on the court to win, to take something. But if you don't care about the outcome, you can't lose; you can only win. If you go out and give your all, you're totally free. It doesn't matter to you. When you finish the match, you're just as happy if you win or lose. Most people want to win because it will make them happier. That adds pressure because they're demanding something back. But if you're perfectly willing to go out and lose, then if it's fine to lose, it's sure as hell fine to win. It's a different attitude and it's very freeing.

I remember seeing Chris Evert playing Martina Navratilova in an exhibition match and she just whomped her. They asked Chris afterward why she did so well. She said, "Well, it didn't really count." You see? You've got to play every match like it doesn't count, full out. Then you've got it.

"The idea is to be in the state of total satisfaction. You don't need anything. If you go out there and don't need anything, you can play very powerful tennis because no one can beat you. You can't lose."

—SALLY HUSS

"You are powerful when you're relaxed because the energy is flowing through you. As soon as you tighten up in any way, you cut that flow of energy."

—SALLY HUSS

"If you can just let your body be free, it will do for you better than what you think you can do yourself."

—SALLY HUSS

Gene Scott

U.S. Open semifinalist

If you consider the old adage "You don't change a winning game," nothing may be further from the truth. When you're playing against a good player, you do have to change a winning game. He's changing his game to adapt to what you're doing, so you'd better be ready to change your game. That's the first observation. The second thing is how to get back to whatever your stability range is. Doesn't the player wish he knew! If he knew, that short lapse, the walk by the wayside, would be very limited.

The players try all sorts of gimmicks. They have little conversations with themselves. They try to focus; they put towels over their heads at the changeovers. John McEnroe might rail at an umpire and try to blame an external force on the fact that his opponent is doing better. No matter how bad he is, the player at the top level doesn't want to be embarrassed. So if somebody's winning or coasting, even if he's a bozo, he's making an adjustment to try to keep the match close.

One of the really terrific things about tennis is it's all there. You give me a fat guy and I can tell him how to play. You give me a guy who's skinny and I can tell him how to play. There's a strategy for everybody on how to beat Pete Sampras. It may not be successful, but there is a strategy for every match.

If you know you're out of shape, naturally you go for big winners. If you know you've got unbelievable legs that could last forever, you bunt back and try to engage your opponent in long rallying exchanges. If the player is competitively better, you try to take percentage tennis out of the deal. You try to be like the backgammon doubling cube. You try to make the game more of a risk. That is exactly what you'd like to reduce the match to. You want to make it more of a game of chance, a matter of luck.

If a player is going to play Sampras and he's got a big serve of his own, he makes sure that if he hits the ball hard, he doesn't hit the ball straight at Sampras. He makes sure that he goes for a line. If he makes the serve, he wins the point. He's not just coasting the ball in the center of the court and encouraging Sampras to rally. That's reducing the percentages in Sampras's favor.

When a player who's winning goes off the mark against somebody he's supposed to beat, the chances are his opponent did something to change his own game. It wasn't a matter of this guy just collapsing. Usually it's the other guy making the adjustment more than a lack of concentration.

The players blame themselves for that all the time. They tell themselves, "Oh, I've got to concentrate; I wasn't focused." That's baloney. That little dialogue with himself is more of an excuse to the audience and to his opponent than it is to him. If it is, it's a self-serving version that has no meaning.

This is mainly caused at the top level by his opponent making an adjustment, not because of his lapse of concentration.

Focus

These players know they're trying to get their first serve in all the time and if all of a sudden they've been coasting in a match and it becomes close, they're going to start to press. They start taking more risks. They think, "Gee, I was winning this match really easily; why aren't I winning it easily anymore?" A concentration lapse is overrated, unless the guy's a total goofball.

CHAPTER FIVE

Pressure

"Pressure is a privilege."

—Billie Jean King,
winner of a record twenty
Wimbledon championships

Michael Chang

In 1989, by winning the Fench Open at age seventeen, became the youngest male Grand Slam champion in the Open era

There is no pressure until you win a Grand Slam, unless you're in a situation like Goran Ivanisevic, where you've accomplished so much and come so close so often that people wonder when you are ever going to win a Grand Slam.

I didn't have that pressure until after I won the French Open. It was tough. Nothing people can say to you will prepare you for how to handle that. It's an experience that you can only go through, something you learn from. I think people forget that the mentality changes.

Ironically, the French Open was only my second career title. Not only are you a seventeen-year-old nobody wants to lose to, but the mentality changes and you're the seventeen-year-old French Open champion who everyone wants to beat. When people play you, they are no longer afraid to lose; they feel like this is an opportunity to beat a Grand Slam champion.

You have a lot of press and public interest, and the mentality was for me to start winning every other tournament. At that point in my career and tennis game, I wasn't ready to do that. In certain aspects, it was very difficult. I learned a lot from it. It helped me down the road.

They were all waiting for me to lose at Wimbledon. The funny thing is, after the French Open, I walked into Wimbledon and I said, "All right, this is the next one." That's part of the innocence and the fire that comes from being a seventeen-year-old. You don't have fear. That's one of the treasures that we sometimes lose over periods of time because suddenly we have a greater understanding of all these things that are actually going on.

"Whenever you go back to places where you've had success, it is always a good feeling because it brings back positive memories and your attitude seems to change. It's fair to say that for most players, when they go back to places they enjoy, they tend to do the best. For me, Paris is one of those places."

—MICHAEL CHANG

Bill Bond

Head tennis pro, La Jolla Beach
and Tennis Club, California

Hitting the ball is one thing, but doing it under pressure is another. Obviously, doing it under pressure requires a little more than mere fundamentals and simple concentration on the ball; there are other things involved. These include your opponent, the circumstances, the score, the weather, the wind, and how you're feeling. Pressure is a different aspect of the sport. It's something that has to be dealt with separately.

You have to have your game in order. Your shots have to be there. You have to have spent your time doing your homework on the practice court; that's number one. You have to be very physically fit. As far as the mental game, it's the feeling that you have the tools, that it's within your ability to win. You have to be able to take that attitude to the tennis court. Part of it is doing it over and over.

One of the things that's important, of course, is to win. Tennis is a game of going up the ladder. You progress all the way up the levels of play until you get to the ultimate level. Each time you climb a step on the ladder, you have to overcome some obstacles mentally. Maybe it's just to beat the people who represent that next level. Once you beat those people, you feel like you're there, and then you start reaching up again. At the highest level of the game, you're shooting for the person who is ranked ahead of you. Until you beat that person, your confidence is not completely established.

Roy Emerson once told me that until he won Wimbledon, he never thought he was any good. That was unbelievable, but that was how he felt. You have to lift yourself up psychologically to accept the challenge of doing what's necessary to beat the person who represents the next step.

"A win over good competition is where mental toughness starts. Once you have some winning under your belt, you enjoy it and you want to maintain it, so that further motivates you to be an even better player."

—BILL BOND

"Jean-Claude Killy once told me that in a pressure situation during the Olympics, he would say to himself, 'I've done everything I can to prepare for this race. If I win it, great. If I don't, my friends will still be my friends, my enemies will still be my enemies, and the world will still be the same.'"

—MARK McCORMACK,
described by Sports Illustrated *as "the most powerful man in sports"*

Richard Leach

University of Southern California tennis coach

Tennis is the cruelest game in the world. There are no time clocks. You can't stall and win like in other sports. You're on your own. There are no substitutions if you're starting to play like you never played the game before. You either win or you lose. There are no rain outs in tennis. That's why it's such a tough game.

It would be amazing to know what's going on in the minds of players when you see them on Centre Court at the finals of Wimbledon or at the U.S. Open. We've all seen players start to choke from the pressure. Their clothes are off; they're out there nude. There's nowhere to hide. It's one of the toughest things in the world to get yourself back on track. When I've choked, I've never been able to recover from it. I continue to suck air and lose and hate myself.

When my players are doing it, I try to find ways to snap them out of it. The best example is when my son Rick was in the finals of the NCAA doubles championships in 1986. He wanted to win that championship more than anything in the world, which was why he was choking. If he won, he would get a medallion on the banister in Heritage Hall on the USC campus.

He was in the doubles finals playing against UCLA and he was feeling the pressure. His partner was a senior, Tim Pawsat. They were a great doubles team, always ranked number one in the U.S. Juniors, but Rick was having a terrible day.

Finally, when I saw him playing so badly, I did something that I'd never done before. We've always had a great relationship and I never spanked him or raised my voice when he was a kid growing up, so all of a sudden I said, "You are playing like a girl. You may as well put a dress on; you're just embarrassing yourself and me." He couldn't believe what I was saying. What I did was to appeal to one of his emotions that was stronger than his choking.

He looked at me and said, "Well, you're a lot of help. Why don't you just get the hell out of here?" And I said, "I am. I can't take anymore. I'm out of here." Now he was so upset with me that he forgot to choke. He started playing like he could play and death was quick for UCLA.

Tennis players are always looking for an excuse to lose. There's a huge fear of losing. They all want an excuse beforehand. So when they're playing, if anything goes wrong, like a bad call by the umpire or a lucky shot by their opponent, now they have an excuse.

They get out of what I call the "circle of concentration." I want to keep them in the center of that circle, but they're looking for a way to get outside. Now they can throw the match and after the match say, "Well, Coach, how could I have possibly won? The guy cheated me!" I've got to keep them inside of that circle so they have no excuse.

Picture a large circle and these guys are straying outside of it and I'm trying to push them back in there. The way to do that is to look at your racket strings and straighten the strings rather than letting your eyes wander to the stands, the spectators, or your opponent. That's what Sampras does. Don't let your mind wander. You want to stay focused on what you're doing.

At Wimbledon, I'll go into the weight room and see all the players working on getting stronger after their matches. You can't appreciate the way they hit those balls by watching it on television. When you watch tennis on television, it looks like the court's just a little skinny thing. I mean, I know how big that court is. Players run from corner to corner to corner. They hit the crap out of the ball.

Also, since Wimbledon is a Grand Slam, the players have a tendency to choke. If you can say you won a Grand Slam, you can walk around pretty proud. There's a different level on the tour events versus a Grand Slam. I just hate to see anybody choke because I know how it feels. But I'm doing it in front of nobody and they're doing it in front of everybody.

Your fate is all in your hands. Once your hands go, you're dead. In other sports, you just run harder or hit somebody and you're okay. In tennis, you have to have control of your hands, and once those go, you're just toast. It's easier in doubles because you have somebody to lean on. But in singles, you're bare. That's why singles is so tough. It's the cruelest game, no question. There's no game that even compares with it.

I get a kick out of golf. I know it's a pretty tough game, because I play it, too. In golf, you're playing against the course. You know how kiss-ass everybody is. They fix each other's divots and give them little claps. Well, that's because they're playing against the course. I want to see them go against each other.

Tennis players won't speak to each other. They get these grudges going. One of the most amazing things is to be in the number one locker room at Wimbledon and watch these guys before they go out on Centre Court in front of millions of people. The Australians are over in one corner of the locker room. The U.S. kids are in another corner. All of a sudden, this British guy in a suit appears and says, "Rafter, Agassi, five minutes." Just the last name. Then these players grab their bags and march out of there one behind the other. I give those guys a lot of credit to be able to deal with that. It just amazes me.

"I feel like I'm stronger than I've ever been, I'm fitter than I've ever been, and I'm moving better than I've ever moved. That allows me the luxury of taking a three-out-of-five-set match and turning it into a sprint, really making every point important, putting so much pressure on my opponent that they have a long ways to go. Whether I'm down or whether I'm up, I now have the platform to execute my game and not to waver from it."

—ANDRE AGASSI,
Wimbledon champion

Pam Shriver

*As an amateur, lost to Chris Evert in the finals of
her first U.S. championships*

I looked at pressure as the enemy. I hated it. I wanted to feel free. When I got tight and felt pressure, I wasn't free. I never got to the point where I didn't feel pressure.

The closest I got was when I was feeling absolutely as confident as you can feel. Then there was very little pressure. Or, when I played a higher-ranked player and I was playing well, then I didn't really feel that much pressure. You're not expected to win and now you're giving her a good run. But you start to feel pressure if you get into a winning position, and then you have some nerves.

"It's not the physical component that makes you feel pressure; it's all about what's going on up in your mind."

—RICK DRANEY,
champion wheelchair-tennis player

"Pressure, I don't want pressure! Give me a nice nineteen-minute match."

—MARY CARILLO,
*television commentator and
former professional tennis plyer*

Jack Kramer

Played in three Davis Cups (1939, 1946, 1947)
with a perfect singles record of 6–0

Davis Cup adds another dimension of pressure. There's a buildup of anticipation that exceeds the excitement of going to the U.S. Open or Wimbledon. The poor captain is supposed to keep everybody relaxed, but he's also supposed to keep everybody practicing. He's a combined coach and psychologist and pal.

Some players react well to having that kind of support, and some players think, "I've gotten here all on my own and all of a sudden I have this high-profile person in the game and he's trying to help me, but all he's doing is mixing me up." The idea that they have this captain who is in charge is a hard thing for some players to handle.

To me, the big difference in Davis Cup over anything else is, when you lose, you haven't just let you, your family, your coaches, and your sporting goods company down, you've let your whole country down. That's the toughest weight you can carry.

"Davis Cup play really affects a competitor because you know that you're playing for a greater cause. It's not just for you. It's the most rewarding and thrilling thing to compete for something greater than yourself."

—TODD MARTIN,
member of U.S. Davis Cup teams, 1994–2001

"Every time I played Davis Cup, the fact that I was representing the United States made it a special deal. If you play a lot of Davis Cup, it gets a little bit easier, but the fact that you're representing your country never goes away."

—DENNIS RALSTON,
seven-time U.S. Davis Cup team member,
four-time Davis Cup captain

"Davis Cup is the greatest pressure of the game. It's greater than a Wimbledon final or a U.S. Open final because suddenly they put USA on your back, and you're carrying the country. The country doesn't know it, but you do!"

—BUD COLLINS,
tennis columnist for the Boston Globe

Ray Benton

Veteran tennis marketer and
cofounder of ProServe Inc.

Tennis is very personal compared to a team sport. There are no excuses. You have the total responsibility of losing and the total responsibility of winning. That greatly ups the ante. When I was president of ProServe, we represented many superstars, and we discovered that tennis players by far have the biggest egos. But they have to. Michael Jordan can walk on the court, score fifty points, and his team can lose. He can score twenty points and his team can win. It's the same for an NFL quarterback. He's got a helmet on, so there's much less risk of embarrassment. It's not personal. Tennis is so damn personal. They have to have much stronger egos.

Tennis and golf have literally only one thing in common: a little hand-eye coordination, but mostly it's the fact that they happen to be the two country-club sports. That's the only thing they have in common. They require totally different emotions. They both have roots as upscale, elite sports. Let's face it, adrenaline helps you in tennis, but it kills you in golf. It just happens that upper-middle-class people play those two sports, so they constantly compare them.

Another tyranny of tennis that probably applies more to the pros than anyone else is that there's an absolute, quantifiable ranking in tennis. You're either number one in the world, or you're number six in the world, or you're 29th in the world, or you're 175th. There's nothing subjective about it. It's a very fair system. It may not be exactly right, but it's there.

Think of this: You're a tournament director in Washington, D.C., and it's a big-deal place with a sophisticated audience. Potential tennis fans will say, "I'm not going to that tournament; none of the top five guys in the world are playing." How many times do you think they go to a basketball game and none of the top five basketball players in the world are playing? Or a football game? Because everybody's good and everybody has their own definition and hype, it's not absolute. The pressure is unbelievable.

Think about all the arrogant trial lawyers you know. How much cocktail-party chatter do you hear, "Oh, he's the best in the world"? How many lawyers in the world walk around thinking they're the best in the world? Let's say 300 of them do, maybe more. Think what would happen if there was a ranking. You'd have a lot of drinking going on by number 100 when he goes to a cocktail party and number 70 is there.

Or take quarterbacks. "He's the best under pressure." "He's the best thrower in the game." "He's the best team leader." Everybody has a way of holding up his ego. Try having a quantifiable ranking. Some of this also goes on at the local level. You're either the club champion or you're not. And it's posted on the board. You got beat in the semifinals, so you're not as good as the guy who won.

Tennis is a very absolute sport and it puts a lot of pressure on the players. It's fascinating to me because we've represented players in every sport and all tennis players are so arrogant. I despise professional tennis players, yet I'm in total awe of them. Think of those guys out there for four hours at the U.S. Open. They've lost the match or they've won the match. They can't hide. They can't say, "Screw you." They're playing naked.

"You can have a certain arrogance, and I think that's fine. But what you should never lose is respect for others."

—STEFFI GRAF,
won all four Grand Slam championships in 1988

"I'm not cocky and arrogant. I'm confident and I tell the truth."

—VENUS WILLIAMS,
ranked number three in the world in 2001

Tony Trabert

International Tennis Hall of Fame

Pressure disappears once you shake the nerves from the first game. From that point on, all you're thinking about is what you're doing on the court. You're not thinking about your winning speech or that you're going to be Wimbledon champion or U.S. Open champion. That's the only way you can deal with it properly.

The first time I played Wimbledon, I was nineteen. I played on Centre Court and I could hardly breathe I was so scared. The net looked higher than the backstop. I lost in straight sets to an Englishman and from then on, when I went out there, I was just fine. I had not gone through that experience before and I'd heard so much about it. That's one of the things you learn. That's part of the mental capacity. You prepare yourself and once you get out there, you shake your nerves.

I never believed in a slump unless you were hurt or just dog-tired because you'd played too much. If you understand the mechanics, the major parts of a forehand or backhand, and you're missing a lot of them, you say, "Let's watch the ball, get the racket ready, keep the wrist firm, watch my contact point." There are only four or five major things. You can discover which one you're not doing, incorporate it, and off you go again.

Golf may be different. If Tiger Woods can play the way he can play and win the Masters by twelve strokes and then three weeks later, he can't keep it in the fairway, obviously there is more to golf than there is to tennis. I never experienced that in tennis. Once I was good, I could stay pretty good. It shouldn't vary. Tennis is a form sport. If you're a little better than I am, you're going to beat me a majority of the time. It may be 7–5 in the third, it may be 6–4, 6–4, but you're going to beat me most of the time. You're not going to beat me every time. But it is a form sport.

Fred Stolle, with whom I work a lot on Channel 9 Australia, says that when you play a Grand Slam tournament, you know you're going to have one bad match. I say, "Bull, why is that?" What if I play six good matches and I'm in the finals and I wake up and say, "Uh-oh, I haven't had my bad match yet in this Grand Slam tournament." Why do you have to have a bad match? Then I recite again, "I didn't have a bad match when I won those three Grand Slams without losing a set." I just never believed in that. Why do you have to have a bad match? You don't if you're prepared and you give it some thought.

Cliff Buchholz

*All-American at Trinity University and twenty-year
director of the Ericsson (formerly Lipton) Open*

When Rod Laver got nervous or was in a pressure situation, he just made sure he kept his feet moving. He knew if he kept his feet moving, that would relax his body and he'd stay loose. He called it "happy feet." As soon as his feet stopped moving, you could see the concrete set in.

When other players get tight, they think about watching the ball. They really watch the ball as closely as they can and they think about watching the ball. They catch the ball early. Some players, on the return of serve, will watch the server and zero in on the ball about the time it hits the ground. Others, when they're really concentrating, will watch the ball in the server's hand before he or she throws it up and then watch it all the way through its entire flight.

Everybody has to find a tool to keep them relaxed. It's a little bit like depression, in that everyone can suffer from depression, but most people find what they have to do to avoid it. Maybe they schedule an hour by themselves, take off a weekend, go for a run, or do push-ups, whatever positive thing they need to do to maintain their equilibrium during difficult times. Tennis is the same way. You need to find out what it is you have to think about during those times of pressure. The good tennis players do.

Chico Hagey

U.S. amateur champion

When I played my absolutely best tennis, it was all psychological. I would go through a streak for a while thinking I was just unbeatable. I would welcome a tight spot. There were two occasions in my life when I went into that streak. One was when I was playing so badly that I dropped any fear of losing. I thought I'd seen the bottom and it wasn't really that bad. I would go out and start playing recklessly. That's when I went to the finals of the NCAA. I had been as low as number thirteen on our team and I rose to number two in collegiate tennis that year among all players.

I lost to the number one player on our team because I *thought* I was supposed to lose to him. I was winning the match fairly handily, then I started thinking about the day before the match when a friend of mine had commented that he thought I was playing well, but he thought the other guy was playing better. It drove me crazy; I thought about it way too much.

The other instance was when I won the amateur national grass-court championship because the receptionist at the tournament said to me, "The moment I saw you, I knew you were going to win this tournament." That little comment by a person who knew nothing about tennis gave me this feeling of luck and I won the tournament. It gave me a sense of invincibility. I felt like I was supposed to win, so I won.

I remember when Bjorn Borg's coach told me that when things start to go wrong, Bjorn first started concentrating on watching the ball. If that didn't work, he paid particular attention to his feet; he wanted to always keep his feet moving.

The other thing I learned was when I was watching Bjorn play a match in Boston. For four points in a row, he had bad luck. He was up 40–love and his opponent hit the ball and it took a bad bounce on the clay; the next point the ball hit the edge of the tape and took a funny bounce; then Bjorn hit the net cord going down the line; and finally there was a bad line call.

Bjorn had four cases of bad luck in a row and at that point in a big game, a lot of us would say, "Well, we're supposed to lose. God has decided we're supposed to lose." But it didn't bother Bjorn at all. He won the next three points, and went on to win the match. I remember thinking, "Don't interpret signs."

"It boils down to a few moments. When you get that one chance and you seize it, it's very satisfying."

—ANDRE AGASSI,
won his first Grand Slam at Wimbledon in 1992

Betsy Nagelson

Ranked as the world's top junior player in 1973

I personally did better when I was playing people I liked, such as a good friend. There wasn't any extra baggage that came onto the court. I wasn't trying extra hard to beat them to prove a point. I wasn't competing for the wrong reason.

When you play someone you like, you can eliminate all that garbage that goes on and just play the point to play the point. You get into a more humbled state of mind that allows you to perform to your ability without all that other stuff. To me, this is an amazing sort of dichotomy.

The sports psychologist, or life in general, teaches you that you cannot win unless you are totally confident and you believe you're better than somebody else. I personally had my best performances when I had a humbled state of mind. I didn't tell myself I was any better than anybody else was. It wasn't about that. I was playing well and it was like a blessing.

When I wasn't playing well, as opposed to beating myself up, I would say, "Well, that's all right. I don't necessarily have these unrealistic expectations. I'm doing my best and I can't ask for anything more." The judgment I placed on myself was lessened. I think there is some truth to that.

Pressure

"Being humble doesn't mean you're weak."

—MARTINA NAVRATILOVA,
International Tennis Hall of Fame

"You can never meet everyone's expectations. It's hard enough to meet your own."

—ANDREA JAEGER,
*Won her first professional tournament
when she was fourteen years old*

Ed Ames

Outstanding recording artist whose hit records
include "Try to Remember"

W hen you start to lose your edge, slow down. Slow
everything down. Try mightily to put it out of your
mind. Don't dwell on it. I'm not saying that you'll be successful at doing this all the time, but that's what I try to do.

You make the concerted effort to say, "That point is
over; let's move on." It's point by point that you win. Give
yourself a little more room for error. In other words, don't
try to hit so deep or hit so close to the line. Stay a little
closer to the middle until you get grooved again and hope
you pull out of it.

"I learned along the road it's not how hard you hit the
ball, but how you hit it and where you hit it. Tennis is
a big head game."

—ED AMES

John Steel

*All-time-winningest player at number one
(Dartmouth) in Ivy League history*

Anybody who has ever played gets little butterflies. You use pressure to give you the energy to go out and beat the other player. They will only start to slip away if you aren't focused on the issue at hand, which is hitting the ball and implementing the game plan. There's always a strategic plan to beat the other person.

When I warm up with somebody, I'll hit him a couple forehands, high and low, and I'll hit him a couple backhands, high and low. I really try to assess what he does well and what he does poorly. If I have someone who has a great forehand and a really poor low-slice backhand, I can tell you he's not going to see many forehands in the match.

Tennis is funny that way. If you go out and you play good defense and you're relatively within 90 percent of the other guy and you don't lose your head and you stay within the game plan, you'll beat the other guy nine times out of ten.

That's how I played. I used to win those tournaments when I was eighteen, nineteen, twenty years old and they'd say, "Steady, unspectacular John Steel won another tournament in a boring way." I thought that it was good to be steady and unspectacular; I didn't see it as boring.

Scott Bondurant

*Captain and two-time NCAA tennis team champion
at Stanford*

When you're in a really tight situation, my sense is always to play aggressive. It's human nature if you're playing a long rally to get uptight, and you can choke. But if you're playing aggressively, if you're going for hard serves, if you're charging, you don't have time to choke. That's how I always handled the tight situations, tight points.

When you're playing well in your head, you always want to play reasonably fast. I remember hardly taking any time at a changeover. It keeps the pressure on the other player. The flip side of that is if things aren't going well, you do the reverse. You take longer between points, between games.

You also try to vary your game. If you have been playing conservatively, you go for more shots. If you get behind, you poach more or you start throwing up a lot of lobs. You do anything you can to change the tempo.

"We tend to overanalyze a lot of things in this sport."

—Pete Sampras,
*ranked number one in the world a record six
consecutive times (1993–1998)*

120

Jim Verdieck

*University of Redlands tennis coach for thirty-eight
years and winner of eleven NAIA and three NCAA
Division III national championships*

As a coach, you are constantly trying to create a pressure situation. Everything was predicated on the pressure matches. Our basic challenge was the nine-game tie-breaker. If you win, you win; if you lose, you lose. What's so difficult about that? That was the pressure cooker. All you do is put them in that position. You give them the opportunity and if they do it and survive, they learned something.

All my coaching was predicated on pressure, pressure, pressure. If you have enough pressure and you survive, and you win, then you must have learned how to handle the pressure.

"We had a Commitment Award at the University of
Redlands. A couple of my alums wanted to have a
Sportsmanship Award. I said, "That doesn't win; it's the
commitment that wins. It's the idea that no matter how
good you are, you dedicate yourself to be better."

—JIM VERDIECK

"My whole philosophy is predicated upon if I find out
why you lost, tomorrow we may be able to fix it."

—JIM VERDIECK

Dennis Ralston

French Open and Wimbledon doubles champion

The first time I played Wimbledon, all the American pros were over there. They all told me not to look around the stands if you go on Centre Court because it's the kiss of death and you'll freeze from the pressure. I listened to them.

I was seventeen and I never once looked at the stands. They would tell me horror stories of guys who would go out and see all 14,000 spectators and they just couldn't play. So I just never looked. Later on I got so I could look around, and that made it more fun.

"In a match, Roy Emerson would twirl his racket constantly. That was his ritual. If you'd said to 'Emmo' that you can't twirl your racket, he wouldn't have been able to play."

—DENNIS RALSTON

Gene Scott

Columnist for the Moscow News

I like the old tiebreaker, the original one that was the nine-pointer. There really was a sudden death to it. In 1970, the first tiebreaker that came out was a five-out-of-nine tiebreaker where at 4-all, the server who had the last three serves got to serve one point. The winner of that point won the set. There was a real finish line. For the spectators, it was unbelievable.

The players who have expressed that they are the vanguard of sports revisionism ran like hell when they were faced with that much pressure. They just said, "No, we don't want it." People still call this sudden death. It's not; there's no finish line. You have no idea technically how long this can last.

For the player, there was a lot of pressure, but that's what you're supposed to have. The players association said, "No, this is too much pressure; we've got to get rid of this." So they changed it to the six-pointer and you had to win by two. Nonsense.

"The tiebreaker ends quicker; the torture ends quicker. That may be why I like to have the tiebreaker because if you're going to be tortured, you want it to be over soon."

—PAM SHRIVER,
seven-time Wimbledon doubles champion

"I love tiebreakers. They bring a match to a crescendo. It's the moment of truth. It's the final seconds of a tie game. It's the last play. It's when the bullfighter's got to go out there and thrust the sword into the bull. Somebody's going to get stabbed. I think it's incredible."

—CHARLIE PASARELL,
chairman and CEO of Indian Wells Tennis Garden, California

CHAPTER SIX

Facing Fears

*"I have an unbelievable
fear of losing."*

—PETE SAMPRAS,
winner of a record thirteen
Grand Slam championships

Jack Kramer

First executive director of the Association of Tennis Professionals (ATP)

I never had a fear of losing. I always used the word *hate*. I hated to lose. The winners are the players who refuse to get beat because they hate the feeling of walking off the court and then spending the time waiting to get out there again.

Normally, in a tournament setting, the wait can be anywhere from three to seven days, and you carry that feeling with you until you're back on the court. That feeling that you hate so much makes you play better to keep from having it.

"If you're afraid to lose, you might as well not play. Nobody likes to lose. Nobody likes to deal with the emotions and feelings that come with losing. But that's part of it and it has to be dealt with."

—RICK DRANEY,
wheelchair-tennis champion

Dick Gould

Stanford University tennis coach with seventeen collegiate national championships

Fear is not an easy thing to overcome. Number one, every athlete gets nervous. In fact, I don't like the word *nervous;* I like the word *excited.* It's a little more positive. *Nervous* to me connotes worried about losing. *Excited* means excited about playing the next point, looking forward to it, and the adrenaline is the same.

Fear of winning might come from setting your expectations so high that you can't meet them every time. I have players who quit the game at sixteen years of age because they'd won everything there was at that time and all of a sudden they lost a match or two and they couldn't stand the pressure of having to win every time they went on the court. It was almost better to lose some, but once they started losing, they couldn't stand that either.

Is there a fear of losing? I hate to say it that way. Perhaps some great athletes feel that way, but I would say that ideally the best athlete is one who wants that ball, who wants to take that shot, who wants the opportunity to make the catch. They want the ball thrown to them; they love that pressure. You have to understand that you don't always win. The best batter in baseball fails two-thirds of the time. Failure is a part of the game.

Sometimes goal setting enters into it. You can set your goals too high or too low. I like intermediary goals that you can reset, rather than big, big goals. I think you should focus on improvement rather than on the result. In other words, in practice, I'll be working on a guy's forehand and he'll run wide and hit the ball in the middle of the net and I'll holler four courts away, "Hey, Charlie, that was a great forehand." He'll look at me like I'm crazy and say, "Coach, I hit the ball in the bottom of the net." And I'll say, "Charlie, yeah, but we've been working on your setup with your feet and you really set up well on that ball"—in other words, focus on the parts rather than on the result.

"Some people think failure is the end of the world. Failure should be a challenge. If you don't get knocked on your ass ten or fifteen times in life, you'll never reach your level of excellence."

—NICK BOLLETTIERI,
world-renowned tennis coach

Billy Martin

*UCLA tennis coach and winner of
the French Open mixed doubles*

Some players want to win, but the fear of winning overcomes that instinct of just letting things happen and just performing at your ability level. They may be one and the same, but whether it's a fear of winning or a fear of losing, to me, they're a bit intermingled. It's a tough thing to overcome once you get that into your system. Sometimes you have to get lucky to break out of it. Not just one match can do it; you need a series of things to go your way.

I'm a firm believer that no matter how hard you work, you need a little bit of luck. I've seen it happen with good players and not-so-good players. Sometimes things just happen. It could be an opponent giving you luck when they get tired, and they give you a chance to win the match. Let your opponents help you. Sometimes when they get nervous, they start rushing; they think they've got to get it over right away.

The players who are under control and have their total mental facility try to let their opponents help them. There's a telling point: "Am I going to have to win this match, or is he going to give it to me?" You really have to be under control mentally to be able to realize that.

"The fear of missing the opportunity or not being able to take advantage of the opportunity translates into the fear of winning. You want it so badly and yet, for some reason, you won't allow yourself to let go of it enough to be able to finish it."

—BILL BOND,
U.S. Professional Tennis Association (USPTA)
Master Professional

"Winning is great, but it's the long road to get there that makes it worthwhile."

—STAN SMITH,
member of ten U.S. Davis Cup teams,
with the U.S. winning seven times

"I have complete focus on the fact that every match can be my worst nightmare."

—ANDRE AGASSI,
raises millions of dollars for charity
through his foundation

Vic Braden

*One of the country's foremost tennis teachers and
founder of the Vic Braden Tennis College*

We choose to let our mind wander and when we do our brain really gets screwed up. It has too many things it can consider and it can only send one signal at a time. Mixed signals can only lead to disaster.

There are people, in my opinion, who have a subconscious need to lose. There are certain people who when they get into close matches are so nervous and excited that getting the point over and losing is less painful than what they suffer while they're in that competition. We're studying brain typing right now and winners have a great ability to do the right thing, hit the right shots, find some way to win. The players who lose find some way to lose.

When you listen to a person who says, "Gee, I played well. I only lost 6–4, 6–3," you know you're talking with a loser because a winner would say, "My God, I lost 4 and 3. Can you believe it?" In my mind, they're so like Jana Novotna when she choked at Wimbledon. She started thinking about the outcome. All of the research shows that when you start thinking about the outcome of a match, that's when you start to lose. You have to think about the process.

A player like Pete Sampras, because his brain type is one that's quite smart and very similar to Jack Kramer's brain type, focuses on the strings of the racket. Notice how he never looks up because he can't afford to let his mind wander. When your mind starts wandering or thinking external thoughts, that's when you get into trouble.

"The top players in the world do not fear losing. They hate to lose, but they don't fear a loss. Losers fear losing. They think about it ahead of time. Winners don't consider losing until after they've lost."

—VIC BRADEN

"I don't know where my point of failure is until I fail."

—MARTINA NAVRATILOVA,
*ranked number one in the world
for a record twelve years*

Michael Chang

At age sixteen, became the youngest male ever
to play on Centre Court at Wimbledon

If you're playing not to lose, it's very different than if you're going out and playing to win. You can see it in a person's game; you can see it in the way he carries himself. In his face. All those things play an important role.

You hear players saying, "I've got nothing to lose." When they know they have nothing to lose, they're not thinking about losing. They're thinking about just going out there and swinging away, and a lot of times, that's what happens and they're able to play some of the best tennis of their lives because they don't have any fear.

When you play with fear, you're afraid of missing shots. You're thinking about not missing shots instead of going out and making shots. There's a difference and you can tell, you can feel it. I've had times when I've played not to lose. It happens more often in tight situations, critical situations, and usually I lose.

Sometimes when you're playing, you have the shot you're looking for, but you don't go after it with the kind of authority you normally would. Because of that, you end up hitting the ball a little bit short. You miss your target. You miss your shot. Sometimes you just don't go for it.

Other times when you have confidence and you're out there playing to win, you're thinking, "That's my shot; it's my opportunity. I'm going to go for it, and I know I'm going to make it. I've made it countless times in practice and I'm good enough to make that shot. Even before you hit it, you know it's a winner.

I have different perspectives on the fear of winning. That mentality is different. That mentality is not necessarily going out and trying to be the best you can be. Those players go out with the attitude of, "Tennis is my livelihood; it's what I want to make a living at. I want to make sure I make enough money where I'm comfortable." They focus upon that aspect of it, rather than striving to be the best. There's a big difference.

When you concentrate on just being good enough, but not your best, it becomes very easy to be satisfied. The problem is that when you reach that point, you no longer have the drive to become better. I see that a lot of times with players on tour. They have the capability of accomplishing more and doing better, yet they are just content with where they are. I think it's tragic in a lot of instances.

For me, I've never looked at tennis as being a way to make a comfortable living. I look at it as a talent that God has given me, and it's my job to go out and make the most of that talent and be the best that God intended for me to be. That perspective alone will help you not only on the court, but off the court as well, because now you have a goal that you're shooting for.

"There's a double fear. Sometimes there's a fear of winning. I don't know why. It's interesting, though. There's a fear of success. Success puts more burdens on you. You get in a comfort zone of being a top-twenty player and you're happy to stay there and be where you're supposed to be. Somehow the fear of success hits a certain type of person."

—MARK MCCORMACK,
named by Ernst & Young "Entrepreneur of the Year," June 2001

"I drew my strength from fear. Fear of losing. I don't remember the games I won, only the games I lost."

—BORIS BECKER,
youngest Wimbledon champion ever, at seventeen years, seven months

Nick Bollettieri

Bollettieri Tennis Academy, Bradenton, Florida

I think Pete Sampras right now fears losing. He may not tell you that, but that's what I believe. The downfall of being the best in the world is you know you have to compete against yourself. You have to push yourself to another level. It isn't easy to push yourself every day.

I think what's happened here is that Pete is trying to win so much that he fears losing; it's new to him. He had fear at the 2001 U.S. Open. When his eyes got glazed and he didn't look around, that was fear. That was like being pinned in the corner with the tigers coming at you. He feared that—not knowing whether or not he could battle it out.

In his book, track star Michael Johnson said, "I don't want to catch the dragon, I want to kill the dragon." That says it all for life. Most people are satisfied in just catching the dragon.

"The fear of losing is a problem every player has to face. The fear of losing is that you're too protective of what you've accomplished; you need to keep trying to reach for more."

—BILL BOND,
master tennis professional,
La Jolla Beach and Tennis Club, California

Todd Martin

Tennis Magazine's *Comeback Player of the Year,*
1999

I'm certainly not afraid of losing. I've lost pretty much every week of my career. I don't think it's a fear of losing; I think it is a fear of winning. It may not even be a fear of winning so much as it is a fear of being in the position to win. If you're in the position to win, then you put yourself in the position to fail.

If you just go out there and you lose, the other guy just beats you. But if you go out there and you get up two sets to love, or you're serving for the match and then the tide starts to turn, it was all just a tease. You were there, you had it, and now it's slowly slipping away. And you can see it slipping away. It's so aggravating.

When I experienced it—in the semifinals of Wimbledon in 1996 against Mal Washington and in the second round of Wimbledon in 2000 against Andre Agassi—it was set off by a miss. It wasn't like all of a sudden I realized I was ahead and my plate changed immediately. I missed a shot that I would just never miss and I just couldn't fathom missing, yet I missed it. I missed it because I missed it, not because I was already tight, but once I missed that shot, that made me tight.

That fear creeps in when I'm not executing what I've so easily executed over the years. All of a sudden my body just doesn't feel the same. During changeovers, when I sit down,

I can feel myself shake a little, when usually I'm pretty calm during the changeover. Somehow an erasing of the mind needs to occur. I don't know if any sports psychologist has figured out how to do that.

The easiest way to stop it is not to let it happen. I think the greats of our sport stop it before anybody else knows it's happening. I'm sure Pete Sampras has had a little bit of locking up over the years during certain matches. One thing that helps him is, he's so athletic that he can change the way he plays, rather than make it a strategic and thoughtful process. He can just tell himself that his mind is getting in the way, so why not just make some big serves, charge the net, and jump around a bit. Whereas others of us honestly feel like if we try to do something like that, we're just going to end up deeper in trouble.

"Your mind-set when you're not favored is more of an understanding that the person you're up against is expected to win by the bystanders. Ideally, you're not affected by what the bystanders think, but most of us are."

—TODD MARTIN

Bud Collins

Author of Bud Collins' Tennis Encyclopedia

There's a fear of winning, particularly for the oldest players and the youngest players. The older players get the yips at some stage and the younger players reach a point where they've never been before. They might have a lead of 5–2 in the fifth set but just can't finish it off.

I think it's a fear of winning. Or it's the feeling that they've never been in this place before, so now what do they do? They're within reach of a title or a match or an upset and suddenly there's a little bit of choking, a fear of winning. They don't quite know how to proceed. With experience, that diminishes.

You also see this fear in older players who are doing things they didn't think they still could do and when they get close to winning, they start thinking, "I'm not supposed to be doing this." Or, perhaps, it's a realization that this may be their last chance to win. There are lots of reasons.

"I hate to lose. I've never gotten over that. My hatred and fear of losing even makes me lose sometimes."

—REGIS PHILBIN,
host of Who Wants to Be a Millionaire

Ben Press

U.S. Professional Tennis Association (USPTA)
Master Professional and winner of thirteen
national titles

Ted Schroeder was one of my peers and one of my idols, and for a long time, he was winning most of the tournaments in his division. Ted is about as fierce a competitor as you ever saw; he was super out there.

Winning was routine. He handled the winning, the trophy, and everything just fine. But on those rare occasions when he lost, he was furious with himself. It really bothered him. The fear of losing was his motivation. Winning was very routine, but losing was very painful.

"The possibility of losing never enters your mind. At least not in the minds of any of the good players who I know."

—TED SCHROEDER,
U.S. singles and three-time doubles champion

Betsy Nagelson

Winner of two world mixed-doubles championships

I'm not sure the fear of losing is any stronger than the fear of winning. I think there are truly people who experience fear of success as much as fear of failure. This is what I've learned and I'm forty-five. I just wish I could have figured this out earlier, but I think I probably had both problems. I didn't want to fail and I was scared to death to succeed, because what would that mean?

Fear in and of itself is not a bad thing. The word itself implies that it's something bad. But it's not; everyone has fear. If you don't, you're just kidding yourself. What matters is that rather than suppressing your fear, you need to confront it. Figure out how you can use your fear to empower you in a different direction. I really think that's possible. Fear of failure isn't a bad thing, and fear of success also isn't a bad thing.

Robbin Adair

Boys' and girls' tennis coach, Coronado High
School, California, for thirty-five years

I'm coaching a girl who's a freshman this year and she is just as charming as she can be until she gets on the court. Then a frown comes over her face and I now know why. She has a father who puts her in an unbearable situation. Nothing she does on the tennis courts pleases him. In her case, I've got to get inside her brain and try to teach her the fun side of the game, have her enjoy the game a little bit. I want her to get a thrill out of setting up a point and doing something well, instead of winning.

The fear of winning is not at all uncommon. What happens is, you have a closer in football, you have a closer in basketball; you've got to have that same kind of mentality in tennis. Some kids just naturally get to the point where it's time to win and they are gung ho; they get fired up. Other kids get fired up to get to that point, but when they get there, they then start playing not to lose. They get very cautious, and they lose.

If you get cautious on the tennis court, you lose control of the ball. You have to finish the stroke to be able to control it. Can you imagine Tony Gwynn trying to hit singles and only taking a truncated swing? It would never work. That's what happens to a tennis player. They get worried about winning a point, they don't hit through the ball, and all of a sudden the ball starts going short or it pops up or it goes out. You have to hit through the ball. You have to stay firmly focused on what you're trying to do. You have to go for the win consistently.

"The greatest accomplishment for a player as far as establishing a strong mental game is to be able to overcome the fear of losing. It's to be able to play the best tennis when it's the most difficult, and when there's the most pressure."

—BILL BOND,
U.S. Professional Tennis Association (USPTA) Master Professional

"You work your whole life to try to be the best you can be, even if it's for only one day or one week."

—LINDSAY DAVENPORT,
U.S. Open and Wimbledon champion

Ray Benton

Founder of the Worldwide Senior Tennis Circuit

I don't think any of the top players are afraid of losing. Occasionally they may be and then they lose. But they didn't get there by doing that very often. The Myers-Briggs test measures whether you're an extrovert or an introvert, whether you're intuitive or sensory, whether you're a thinker or a feeler. First, literally every great champion has been an introvert. He gets his energy from within, not from someone else. Second, he is totally sensory in that he totally concentrates on the moment. He totally concentrates on the process, not the result.

In the IMAX movie on Michael Jordan, Phil Jackson points out that in the sixth game against Utah, Michael had missed seven of his previous eight shots. But it didn't even occur to Michael. All that occurred to him was, "Give me the ball and let me execute." He wasn't worried about the past or nervous about what was going to happen in the future if he missed.

Jimmy Connors was down match point to Mel Purcell in Detroit at a senior event. He had never lost to Purcell and he ended up winning it. They had a press conference and a reporter asked, "What were you thinking about at match point?" Connors said, "Nothing." The reporter responded, "Nothing? What do you mean? You were down match point and you had never lost to him." Connors said, "Yeah, but the ball didn't know that."

Facing Fears

If that's the characteristic of champions, fear of losing doesn't enter into it. There's a will to win, but that's in intensity, and in running harder, and I'm sure there's some gamesmanship involved. The Connors and McEnroes of the world didn't try to intimidate; they didn't have to. Agassi does a bit of that now. He looks them in the eye and says, "You know, you're going to have to run from side-to-side for the next four hours if you expect to beat me." That's why he's a much better player than he used to be. He's not worried about what they're going to do. All he's worried about is executing. Somewhere along the way, we've lost our appreciation for tennis, the best damn sport in the world.

"Jimmy Connors was driven more by the fear of losing than by the pure joy of winning."

—TOM GULLIKSON,
former Davis Cup captain

"You just have to be so confident that you can overcome the nervousness."

—LOUISE BROUGH CLAPP,
four-time Wimbledon singles champion, five-time Wimbledon doubles champion

Jeff Moore

Fourth women's tennis coach to win more than 500 career matches, University of Texas

I think there's too much emphasis on results and not enough on performance, starting with your preparation. We live in such a sound bite generation. A lot of the players who I recruit are under the impression that they can come here, put in their time, and they'll become an all-American.

What they're not as willing to do is to go through the frustration, the down times, the pain. There's really a lot of pain that goes into anything you do that's special. You're going to have to take risks and go through some tough, tough periods and work through them. That's what our practices are designed to do—put you through the same type of pain you're going to face in a match, and then the matches will be easy.

"Bobby Riggs's desire to win overcame any fear of losing. He never thought about losing. He was just trying to win. There's a big difference. If you get into a match and you're afraid of losing more than you are trying to win, that's a big difference."

—LORNIE KUHLE,
owner of the Bobby Riggs Tennis Club

Randy Snow
Wheelchair tennis champion

I love tiebreakers! I love it when it counts because it's an opportunity to be great. It's the chance, it's the adrenaline. I love the energy.

It's also an opportunity for fear. Players come into those situations and they turn it into fear. It's fear either way; but it's what you do with that fear. Man, I just focus. I push the edges of the court in, and I make the tennis ball as big as I can. These are personal techniques. It's emotional fitness. Who can manage the emotion?

———————

"You need to feel a little bit scared. Not feel fear, but know that anyone can beat you, that it's not like you can just go to the court and know you're going to win. You have to work."

—MARAT SAFIN,
2000 U.S. Open champion

Gene Scott
Member of U.S. Davis Cup team

The fear of losing is the biggest mind-set at Davis Cup and it rises another notch at every match. You play with a fear of losing because you're losing not just for yourself but for your country. It's a double embarrassment. And you don't have double accomplishment.

Davis Cup is best characterized as a survival. It's more, "I got through it. I represented my country and I survived." It's not that you were a star. I never met anybody who ever said, "Gee, I was the star of that Davis Cup." Someone may have said that. But mostly it was, "God, I got through it."

CHAPTER SEVEN

Power versus Tactics

*"I've realized that I've had
to stay strong to keep up
with the power game."*

—JENNIFER CAPRIATI,
gold medalist in singles
at the 1992 Olympics

Michael Chang

First American since Tony Trabert (1955) to win the French Open (1989)

The tactics nowadays are much subtler. Fewer and fewer players employ them. The power aspect of tennis has become more of a strategy now than it has ever been. To get your short ball, you smack the ball as hard as you possibly can, versus working the ball around, opening up the court, using angles, using depth.

It has changed in some aspects, but the strategies these days are much less apparent. They're not as noticeable because everybody hits hard and everybody hits big. You don't have the kind of rallies you would normally have or the manipulation of the ball as much. You don't have guys playing angles as much or playing toward weaknesses. The strategy now is, who can beat whom to the punch?

"You walk off against her, and you don't have the impression you played a tennis match. You feel as if you've been in a tag-team wrestling match or a boxing bout but not tennis. She just bangs away."

—NATHALIE TAUZIAT,
French tennis pro, talking about playing Venus Williams

Tom Gullikson

Pete Sampras's interim coach

I think a classic example of great tennis was the quarterfinal match at the 2001 U.S. Open between Pete Sampras and Andre Agassi. Here were two great champions playing a night match. There was a lot of electricity. Typically, I would watch that match from up in the sponsor suites, but I was right down by the court; I wanted to feel the match. Sampras was playing a classic serve-and-volley-style, attacking-type game. Agassi, with his great return and ground strokes, was playing an aggressive baseline game.

These were completely different strategies, but the one thing they both had in common was that each one held his serve the entire match without breaking. Agassi stumbled a little bit in the tiebreakers and that was the difference. Here were two great players, both formerly number one in the world, playing completely different tactics, yet executing at a very high level. It was some of the best tennis I've ever seen.

Tactics are always going to be part of the game. The only difference now is the technology and the size of the players. These guys are six four and strong, and they do so much more off-court training and weight lifting. The science of being an athlete is far more advanced than it was when we were just doing push-ups and sit-ups and running wind sprints.

In addition, the technology with the rackets has greatly advanced. Now when you're twenty feet off the court and on the run, you can scream a winner down the line. Whereas in the old days, you'd be running on your forehand side and you'd loop the ball back and slow it down to give yourself time to get back on the court. Or on your backhand side, you might hit a nice slice crosscourt to give yourself plenty of time to get back onto the court, where you can hopefully neutralize the guy. That's changing, but the basic principle of hitting it in the court one more time than the other guy to win the point is not going to change.

You can still play pretty good tennis tactically if you're a little guy, but you have to execute really well. I played the tour from 1975 to 1986 and I know when I played Wimbledon in 1977, 48 out of the 128 players were Americans. In 1979, my brother Tim was eleventh in the United States and he was eighteenth in the world. He wasn't even in the top ten in the United States, yet he was eighteenth in the world. It's much more of a worldwide game now. Every country has a tennis federation, and their sole purpose for existence is developing players at their national training centers to supply their Davis Cup teams, their Federation Cup teams, and their Olympic teams.

"I think the best feeling is when somebody pushes you to the limit and you dig down a little bit extra. That can happen with any player. Somehow, it seems to be asked of you more when you play Pete."

—ANDRE AGASSI

"Andre inspires me. I don't care if it's a practice set or the finals at Wimbledon. We bring out the best in each other, and it'll be that way for the rest of our careers."

—PETE SAMPRAS

Vic Braden

Teaching professional for fifty-seven years

I don't think tennis is the mind game it once was. But what's happened sequentially is that the intellectual functioning levels can be quite a bit lower now than in the past. The reason for that is, players are just hitting hard line drives to each other and the ball is usually missed on the third hit. We do all kinds of studies on that. There are not as many tactics right now; it's actually just stroke production, who can hit the ball back the hardest.

What happens on a physics side is you get half of your opponent's speed plus 1.5 times your racket hit speed, so the ball speeds up with each hit. With each hit, your chances of losing increase and on about the third hit, there's usually a mistake. The game has made a radical change from one that needs some intellectual processes to one that only really needs mechanics.

The serve, for instance, is mechanics. If the player serves well, it doesn't matter where he serves. If he serves 135 mph, you're just going to salute it as it goes by. At 135 mph, the ball reaches you in about four-tenths of a second and it takes half of that time just for your brain to send the message for your muscles to move. That's less time to react than if Roger Clemens were pitching to you.

Equipment is by far the biggest change. The rackets are so light now. They have great maneuverability. I remember

Pancho Gonzales, before he passed away, picked up a racket and said, "I just can't believe with these new rackets I'd ever miss a single volley." He played with a fifteen-ounce wooden racket. The game today is twice the speed, half the weight. To get speed, you need a stiff racket, and in the past to get a stiff racket, you needed to put in a lot of wood. Now you have a stiff racket from the new, modern materials and it is also light. It's the best of both worlds.

"When Howard [Head] designed the Prince racket that would change tennis forever, he didn't want it to be merely a fat racket. He wanted it to have lines. He insisted that the throat had to be beautiful; it couldn't just be functional."

—MARTY HEAD,
widow of Howard Head

Donald Dell

Senior vice president, marketing, television, and sports, Clear Channel Entertainment

The men's game is being taken over by power because the equipment is so strong. Frankly, it's more boring. I think you've got to change the game to one serve for each point. You've got to jazz up the game for television on the men's side of it.

The women pros are great because the rackets still do a lot of the work and the women are more attractive and exciting in a lot of ways. There are more good ones today. There are twenty good women players today, but twenty years ago, there were probably only five.

"Some people are just power. Some people are just smarter."

—LOUISE BROUGH CLAPP,
winner of twelve U.S. doubles titles

Jeff Moore

University of Texas women's tennis coach

The women's game is an abomination right now. It's awful. The popularity in women's pro tennis is based on the personalities, but the top women are winning despite having as many as fifty unforced errors in a match. From a purist's point of view, it's not good tennis.

On the men's side, conversely you have players like Andre Agassi, who in his ripe old age is seen as a smart player. He plays aggressively, but he plays intelligent tennis. Basically, he takes what you give him. If you force him to build a point, to play defense, he'll play defense. If you give him a ball that he can work with to attack you, he'll attack you. But he's not going to be on the attack unreasonably. I think the men's game, except for Wimbledon because of the surface, is far more entertaining to watch from a purist's point of view.

In the women's game, there's a collection of four or five players who are bigger and stronger than everyone else, and whoever is on wins. Very few adjustments are made on the women's side. That's not to take away from their mental toughness. Venus and Serena Williams and Jennifer Capriati are warriors. That is their strength.

The problem is, there's so little competition at their level on the women's side that they have not been forced to adapt like the men have to play more intelligently. They can stay in the top five and no one touches them because they're just bigger and stronger, and, more importantly, meaner. The men are like animals in the jungle; there are lions everywhere threatening, so they have to adapt. They're playing more intelligent points.

"They were playing a brand of tennis that I was totally unfamiliar with. The pounding was so concussive and the running back and forth so athletic—everything about that match was so much more ballistic than I could have scared up. I played another sport."

—MARY CARILLO,
television commentator and
former professional tennis player

Ben Press

For twenty-eight years was director of tennis at the
Hotel Del Coronado, California

I'm totally opposed to what's going on now in tennis. They had the National Girls 16s in San Diego. This is the big tournament. They had 190 of the best girls in the country. If you put sacks over their heads, they all play exactly alike. You couldn't tell one from the other. Some just do it a little better than the others. But they all stand back, and they hit the ball as hard as they can with that Western or semi-Western forehand or two-handed backhand. Very few of them volley. Very few of them have any strategy. They just hit the ball hard.

When we "over the hill" guys were playing, and I watched somebody like a Jack Kramer or a Pancho Gonzales or a Ted Schroeder carve up somebody, it was fun. I wrote an article some years ago that appeared in one of the national tennis magazines in which I said, "In my opinion, the worst thing to happen to American tennis was Andre Agassi's success." I'm an Agassi fan; I don't mean it like it sounds. But every kid on the block now wants to hit the ball 300 mph and they don't have that ability.

My concern is that in twenty years, there will be very little senior tennis because these kids who are playing now aren't going to be able to play. Their bodies are just taking too much physical abuse. If you read about a tournament today, there are walkovers, retireds, and defaults. When we were playing, a default was an absolute rarity. A retired almost never happened and a walkover just didn't occur. The game is awfully different now.

"Tennis has never been a more demanding sport, physically and emotionally. Tougher competition and a deeper field means more pressure, which can lead to more stress on the body. Perhaps we need to adjust our expectations and come to grips with the fact that the trade-off for unprecedented power and unprecedented athleticism is an unprecedented incidence of players' injuries."

—JON WERTHEIM,
senior writer for Sports Illustrated

Raquel Gisafre

Former number-one-ranked woman in Argentina and cofounder of Promotion Sports

Power has changed in the men's game and it's changing in the women's. We can see in the case of the Williams sisters that they are so strong physically that they are overpowering their opponents. I prefer the finesse game. I like to work the point out and have a strategy. But the power game has a lot of merit as well.

In the women's game, they still work out the point. You don't see them acing as much as the men do. I hope it doesn't continue to increase, but it could. When they work out the point, it's exciting. There are a lot of players who are playing really well. The rallies are really fast, but they still have rallies. The women don't overwhelm each other with their serve yet.

Todd Martin

Twice president of the Association of Tennis Professionals (ATP) Player Council

Tennis is meant to be a strategic endeavor. It's supposed to be cat and mouse and athletic. It's supposed to have many facets. It's a pity it's going in the direction of power. In history, I feel like there have always been times where something about the sport, the power, or the spin of the shots, took over for a moment. A moment could be six months or a year, maybe longer.

But then the capabilities of each and every other player to endure either that power or that spin catch up and then once again the sport becomes much more tactical. You can't help but occasionally have the physical attributes of the players dominate, but I always feel that in the end, the mind is the most important part of our sport.

Power versus Tactics

"To be a really great tennis player, you have to have power, but you also have to have finesse. The finesse part of the game is related to your ability to get the other person out of that zone where he is focused on the ball and to get him to start thinking. The quicker you get him thinking about something else, the quicker you'll unwind him."

—JOHN STEEL,
all-time-winningest player at number one
(Dartmouth) in Ivy League history

Dick Gould

Stanford University tennis coach with seventeen NCAA championships

The return of serve is such a big shot right now that you can dictate the point with the return of serve. Players used to be content with just pushing the ball back, but now the forehands are so big that if you just push the ball back, the server already has control of the point without even having to stroke a volley. He's going to rip a big forehand.

I used to work on chipping the ball or putting the ball in play on the return, then working to build the point. Now I have to coach my players to do something big with the return.

I think the bigger factor in serving is, in the old days, you had to keep your front foot on the ground. You couldn't leave the ground until after you hit the ball. Nowadays guys are very big and they leap off the ground. They're hitting the ball two or three feet farther inside the court. And the ball is coming at you at 135 mph. It gets there sooner.

In general, the big racket does help on the other shots, but it doesn't make the ball go a lot harder on the serve. I don't think the racket alone has made that big a difference in the game. I think you might find less serve-and-volleyers now because people are returning so well with the big rackets.

Mary Carillo

World Tennis *magazine columnist*

Brad Gilbert owned John McEnroe and Boris Becker. Becker would look over the net and there was Brad chicken-shitting the ball all over the place and not really hitting it. He wouldn't give you anything until you'd come to the net, then he'd give you a little more than you wanted and he'd pass you.

Brad was smart enough to know that he didn't have the gifts of all the other players around him like McEnroe and Becker or whoever else he was torturing. What he knew he had to do was to bring the big boys down to his level and beat them from there. That to me is pure genius. He was able to do that. He'd take them off their game and he wouldn't give them the ball they wanted to hit. He gave them absolutely no pace until the moment when they realized they couldn't handle it. He knew what he was looking for.

He had great court sensibility. It drove guys crazy. He walked on the court and looked like the kind of guy you see in the public park with black socks on. He had an ugly-ass game. Brad was a true thinking player. As a coach, he pretty much implanted his brain in Andre Agassi's head and it changed Agassi's career. Some people are really good at that. Even his book title tells the same story—*Winning Ugly*.

"Brad Gilbert understands the mental part of tennis better than anyone I have ever met."

—ANDRE AGASSI,
ranked number three in the world at age eighteen

"The power rackets give the advantage to the baseliners, the guys who have to return these huge serves—the guys who have to cook up those huge passing shots, the guys who have to run from side to side on the baseline. People gasp when they see little guys with big rackets staying up with the big guys with big rackets."

—MARY CARILLO

"Pete Sampras could be a champion with a two-by-four in his hand."

—MARY CARILLO

Dennis Ralston

Three-time U.S. doubles champion

Pancho Gonzales was the best player who ever played. He was my idol. Pancho said to pound your opponent's weakness and don't deviate from this tacic until he beats you with it. So, if you have a backhand that's not as strong as your forehand, I will keep attacking it. As I was developing my game, I kept thinking, "I can't do that, he's going to know it's going there. Pretty soon, he'll catch on to what I'm doing." But I found if there was a distinct weak side to somebody's game, I was always a lot better off when I had the opportunity to attack that side.

Tennis is fast, and that's why the repetition and the instinctive play is important. When the ball comes to point X, you hit it to Y. Most of the time, you do that as a pattern. The good players are able to change that pattern at the last second if they need to.

I tell players to go with their first instinct or thought as to where they're going to hit the ball. A lot of players change their mind just as they hit the ball. They were going to go down the line and then they change their mind right before they hit it, and go crosscourt and they miss it.

I say, "Did you change your mind?" I'm right 90 percent of the time when I see it as they changed it. They ask how I know that and I say I can just tell, because they changed it too late. They didn't execute either shot. I don't think you can change in the middle of a point and be successful.

Rick Draney

Six-time U.S. Open wheelchair division tennis champion (quad)

Wheelchair tennis is primarily a baseline game. If a player gets into the net, it's far too easy to lob them. They just don't have the height to be able to cover the backcourt. The strategy, the tactics, and developing your strengths to prey on your opponent's weaknesses during the competition is really what it comes down to.

However, as the rackets have improved, as the athletes' abilities have improved, there are more components of pure strength within the game. It hasn't gone as far to the power mode as the able-bodied game has, and I don't know if it ever could get there, because a wheelchair tennis player uses only the upper extremities.

Without the use of your legs, you lose a lot of the ability to generate the speed, power, and pace of the ball that an able-bodied player can. I don't know that it would ever get as extreme as some might think it is in the able-bodied tennis game, but there are some guys who can tee off on it. When they get a shot they like and it's in their wheelhouse, they can crank it pretty doggone good.

Randy Snow

Ten-time U.S. Open wheelchair tennis champion

Wheelchair tennis has become a much more powerful game. We're hitting stronger from both sides. We have power on both sides. The serve will always be limited because we're not as tall. Our trajectory is not there. Plus, in the wheelchair tennis serve, we're not moving. We create momentum and then we negotiate and manage that momentum to the next point. It's important because we're moving.

We're like skaters playing tennis. A skater would rather move through the action and then use that momentum to come back into play. That's more relative to our sport. We're not working the entire time. There's an output, there's a push, and then there's a resting phase. There's a push, which is a working phase, and then a resting phase. It's unique.

Gene Scott

Founder and publisher of Tennis Week

Unless you are a complete idiot, which may help some players, you know that there are crucial times in a match. However, you can't isolate one and say this is it because you don't know what's going to happen the next game. While you're playing, you can't possibly identify what the key point of the match is. That's nonsense. But you can identify what a critical point is and then at the end someone can certainly say, "That happens to have been the key point of all the key points." That's after you examine the dynamics of what happened during play.

Pete Sampras is an unbelievably gifted player for whom there is no key point. He plays all the points the same. I used to take pictures of him. When he won his first U.S. Open as a nineteen-year-old and beat Andre Agassi, I took a picture in the first set, which he won, and then in the last set, which he won. You'd have no idea which one was which. His facial expression was the same.

The way Sampras approached every point was the same. Even though he wasn't thoughtful enough to be a Zen person, that was how he played. There was no such thing as a big point; he played every point exactly the same. That happened to work for him because he was so gifted. Boris Becker was also gifted, but he knew the difference between a big point and a little point. You could tell emotionally, both by your own emotion and by his emotion, how he treated the big points differently. Sampras didn't.

In the women's game, power has become a tactic. Just look at the Williams sisters and Lindsay Davenport and Monica Seles in the beginning. Seles was the first woman to stand on top of the baseline and whack the ball. Jennifer Capriati did it to a lesser extent. She didn't stay on top of the baseline as much. Power as a tactic was first obvious with the women as a pure tactic all by itself.

With the men, it wasn't a tactic; it became part of the improvement of the overall level of play. When I played, there was something called the pusher; you'd just push it over the net. Both the players and the equipment got so much better that there is no such thing as a pusher anymore. A player rallies the ball from the backcourt and he can hit a winner from the backcourt even with his opponent in the backcourt. That couldn't happen twenty-five years ago. There was no such thing. The power didn't become a winning tactic; it just became a style of play that improved the overall level of the game.

What is not measurable with statistics is time and place. Don Budge could hit one great shot 1,000 mph from the backcourt, but, believe me, he could not do it in the multiple repetitions that athletes do today. These guys, from any point in the court, can hit the ball to any place. They hit the ball as hard as they can every shot and they keep it in the court. That was not true twenty-five years ago.

If we hit one ball a season on the baseline with a half-court-volley-like stroke with a lot of power, we'd think that was great. Well, now the players can do it as a matter of course. Again, a lot of it is the equipment, but a lot of it is because they've had the chutzpah to practice it over and over again. They practice year-round. And they're practicing just fooling around how to make this game of multiple repetitions more acceptable in the rallying configuration, which is actually sort of boring.

Players just start to do strange stuff, like whacking the ball from strange positions all over the court using power as a tactic, with different elements like the return of serve. Being able to hit the return of serve as hard as you can with a lot of topspin has made the server stay back. The serve-and-volleyer is becoming more obsolete, but the reason is, the returner has made him obsolete.

Will there be another generation that will make the next step? The server will find something new that will enable him to hop the ball so high to the backhand that the two-hander can't generate enough pace and the one-hander can only slice it back. Maybe that will be the next technique. We've had an incredible evolutionary time frame in bird years, twenty years; Andre Agassi proved you could do it in three years when he didn't play Wimbledon. That's because he adapted to the big servers. He made the return of serve as big as the serve.

CHAPTER EIGHT

The Other Side of the Net

*"My serve is my biggest
weapon. It's like a knuckleball.
It's hard to read the spin.
It just jumps at you.
It's really a trash serve,
but it mystifies everyone.
What can I say? It's in a
league of its own."*

—ALEC BALDWIN,
actor and celebrity tennis player

Tom Gullikson

Doubles finalist, Wimbledon, 1983,
with brother Tim

Tim and I were identical twins. Tim was right-handed and I am left-handed. Tim was in a tournament in California and he was playing Karl Meiler from Germany. I wasn't there. Tim beat him in three sets.

I showed up two weeks later in Memphis in the U.S. Indoor Tennis Tournament. Tim wasn't there. In the third round, I was playing Karl Meiler and I took him in straight sets. After the match in the pressroom, they were interviewing him and he said, "Who is this Gullikson guy? Two weeks ago in California, he beat me right-handed, and today he beat the hell out of me left-handed. If we play two weeks from now, maybe he'll beat me double-handed." He had no idea we were identical twins.

Regis Philbin

Television host of Who Wants to Be a Millionaire

I have played against former president Bush, the father, a number of times. He's a great guy. He always plays in Chris Evert's charity tournament in Florida. The last time we played, he had a serious hip problem. In fact, he played in the tournament and then flew directly to the Mayo Clinic, where they replaced his hip.

So at the tournament, he was limping. But that didn't stop me. I went right for the limp, right for the hip. Let me at him! Let me see him run! He's a great guy. I was playing with Jim Courier against Bush and Chris. Of course, Courier never ran so much in his life, but I was right there protecting my half of the alley all the way.

"My favorite strategy is when my opponent is stuck at the net, and I hit my topspin down-the-line passing shot. He's left looking like a guppy with his mouth wide open. That feels as good as having a superb slice of foie gras."

—BERTRAND HUG,
owner, award-winning Milles Fleurs restaurant,
Rancho Sante Fe, California

Robert Conrad

Only actor inducted into the
Stuntman Hall of Fame

I was playing with Chris Evert in Houston and she was doing the right thing, getting the ball to me. She just wanted the match to look good. She knew she was the better player, not even close, so she was being a softy.

All of a sudden, I saw this opportunity and I smoked her. I really smoked her. She came up to the net and whispered to me, "Not good to do that to Mother Tennis." That was the last time I saw the ball.

That's a true story. And after that, I was done. She walked back to the line and I never saw the ball again. It disappeared on me.

Alan Thicke

Star of the television series Growing Pains

I played in an exhibition match, Chris Evert and I against Barry Gibb and Martina Navratilova, and we were all playing to the crowd. Of course, the real match was between Barry and me because the pros cancel each other out. So the differential is how the two schmucks play.

We were having some fun and it was pretty even when we came to match point. Martina was serving to me and she called out to the crowd, "Should I ace him?" With one voice in unison, as if it's the Christians and the lions and they're all putting their thumbs down that he must die, they all shouted, "Yes!!!"

For the only time that day, I got to see what a real Martina serve was like. I had my hands full with the others, but Martina just reared back and I still haven't seen that ball to this day. You like to think you're actually hanging in and playing the game until that point and they just ratchet it up and you see where the real level of play is. Like I said, I'm still looking for that ball.

"You get a TV show, then you get to play tennis with all the great players."

—ALAN THICKE

Mary Carillo

Winner of the French Open mixed-doubles title with John McEnroe

Playing mixed doubles in my first French Open with John McEnroe was fabulous. The whole thing was ridiculous. It was my rookie year. I'd never been to the French Open before; I'd never even been to France. It was my first swing through Europe. John was in twelfth grade, skipping time in the final months of his high school career because the U.S. Tennis Association sent him over to play in the Junior French Open. He and I had played together a million times before. He was still an amateur and I had just turned pro. We were in Paris together. There was a sign-up for the mixed doubles, so we did.

John looked at the list and he was singularly unimpressed. He said, "Jesus, we should win this thing." And two weeks later, we did. The beauty of it was, I was really choking in the final. We were playing on court central. We were the warm-up for the men's finals, so toward the end of the match—it was a three-setter—the stadium was really filling up. They couldn't wait until our match was over. And I was choking. At that point, John was just like, "Just kick your serve over, get it in, and I'll do everything else." That's exactly what I did and we ended up winning it, 7–6, 6–3.

The funny thing was, the winners got $1600 as a team. That's 800 bucks each, which wasn't bad. But since John was an amateur, he wasn't allowed to take the money. He said to me, "Go and get both of our prize money checks and give half to me." I gave him this withering look and said, "Why should you get half? I'm the pro. Maybe I'll throw you a couple of bucks, but you're an amateur." I was being so mature. What happens, however, is that you get only your half. They won't give you your partner's half. I got my singles, doubles, and mixed-doubles money and he got bumpkin. It was beautiful. That first year was wonderful.

I'm constantly asked, "What is the secret of John McEnroe?" Obviously, he has enormous talent and he had a great concept of the court. He could look at it and see winners that no one else could see. He just saw things and knew how to create points. He knew when he'd hurt you, when to go from offense to defense and then right back to offense again.

The fact that he was short for a long time growing up— we called him "runt" at the Douglaston Club—actually helped him. He never had a huge growth spurt, a huge power spurt. That never happened to John. Even as a pro, he was an unremarkable-looking fellow. He looked like a doughy frat boy. Because he was small, he learned how to play, to put together points, to use his opponents' power against them, and to be very, very quick. He had amazing footwork.

The same year we won the French mixed doubles, we went off to Wimbledon together. John went in as a qualifier, and made it to the semifinals. To the British press, I became the John McEnroe expert, because they obviously knew what his future was going to be like. However, they didn't know what his past was like.

They were asking me, "How does he make that feathery little drop shot?" And I'm saying, "Boys, I've been watching him do that shot since he was eight. You should have seen that shot three years ago. You think it's impressive now! He's been torturing me with that shot for twelve years!"

What John has is almost more artistry than athleticism. He's uncopyable. In almost the same way that Jimmy Connors was uncopyable. Girls copy Chris Evert. Boys copy Bjorn Borg. But Connors used his two hands differently than Borg. He sat right on the baseline and spat the ball back at you before it even reached any kind of bounce, and came down on the ball.

Everyone copied Borg, who was ten feet behind the baseline, throwing in all that topspin. Some people you just can't copy. Martina Navratilova is incredibly pissed off that more people didn't copy her. She'd say, "If I'm number one in the world, why isn't everyone copying me instead of Chris?!" Guess what, it's hard to copy that. Most kids learn from the baseline. Very few of them really have an inclination to come to the net the way the serve-and-volleyers do and that's still true today.

"It was odd growing up next to John McEnroe. Here I was, number one in the East, number ten in the United States, and I was still the number two player at the Douglaston Club. That's depressing."

—MARY CARILLO

"I always dreamed of being a rock star."

—JOHN MCENROE,
International Tennis Hall of Fame

"I kept the trophy because the man on it was really big and the woman was really small. I hope things have changed by now."

—SENATOR HILLARY CLINTON,
*on a trophy she once won in a mixed-doubles
tennis tournament*

Richard Leach

University of Southern California tennis coach

If you look in the *Guinness Book of World Records,* you're going to see my name in there. I played in the longest match in the history of tennis, at the Newport Casino, Rhode Island, with Dickey Dell in doubles. We played Len Schloss and Tom Mozur. One of the sets was 49–47, and another one was 22–20. James Van Alan, who was the inventor of the tiebreaker, was running the place. He was a little bumpkin. He was running around saying, "I tell you, people, we've got to play the tiebreaker. People don't want to watch that kind of tennis. That set was six and a half hours. Who wants to watch that? You've got to have a finish."

Our match kept dragging on until it finally got dark, and at the same time, we ran out of tennis balls. The sporting goods store across the street was closed and it was seven o'clock at night and the big party was that night. The club members, all dressed up, were coming for a big lobster cookout. We were still playing as they began to arrive for the party. They were all watching our match, betting on who was going to lose their serve. Meanwhile, my wife was patiently waiting at the hotel and she had given me strict orders. She said, "The party's tonight, so don't go drink beer with Roche, Newcombe, and all those other Aussies."

When I finally got to the hotel at about seven-thirty and the party had started at six-thirty, she was irate. I said, "I've been playing." And she said, "Yeah, sure you've been playing. You were playing at the bar!" I quickly showered and when we finally got to the party, everybody was talking about our match. She then had to apologize for not trusting me.

The next day, the singles were set to go on at one o'clock and they said, "You guys start at noon on center court. No, maybe you better start at eleven just in case." We then played for another three and a half hours. We finally got to match point on the second day and my partner hit a terrible return, one of about a hundred that day. They smacked the ball at me, I was at the net and it hit the throat of my racket and went over their heads for a winner. I didn't even know the match was finally over. I won it with my throat volley over their heads. The score was 3–6, 49–47, 22–20. Isn't that something? That just shows that if you get four guys who can't return serves, you can play forever.

"When Jimmy Van Alan invented the tiebreaker, he was sick of three-hour matches; it ruined his cocktail hour."

—Bud Collins,
colorful and internationally known television tennis interviewer of Wimbledon champions

Nick Bollettieri

Renowned tennis coach

Andre Agassi was playing Boris Becker in the semifinals in Monte Carlo. I was sitting in the middle of Brooke Shields and Barbara Becker. Boris was losing big and Barbara turned to me and said, "Help him, Nick. You've got to help him."

I said, "Barbara, the camera's on me. I can't coach him; they'll fine me $1,500!" She said, "Go ahead and coach him. I'll pay the $1,500 and throw in a $500 tip."

Pam Shriver

Champion doubles player and now an outstanding television tennis commentator

There are certain matches you always remember. My first major was with Martina Navratilova in 1981. We were playing in the doubles final at Wimbledon and it was on my birthday. We were to play on Centre Court, where they used to have a big standing-room-only crowd all along the left side of the court.

As we walked out, the standing-room-only, knowledgeable British die-hard tennis fans started singing "Happy Birthday" to me. It spread to the whole of Centre Court, which was kind of cool.

"I have a love-hate relationship with tennis. I love to watch it on television, but I hate to run around in the hot sun. They should play tennis only at night."

—STELLA STEVENS,
"the Sexiest Woman on Earth"

"Chasing the top ranking is like chasing a girl. The chase is the fun part."

—JIM COURIER,
former number one tennis player in the world

Jack Kramer

Pioneer of professional tennis in the United States

Bobby Riggs once booked Pancho Gonzales and me into an opera house in Saratoga, New York. Our portable tennis court was seventy-eight feet long and this place was seventy-five feet long. We were so close to the wall that we couldn't bring our racket back. We served the ball and we had to step in because if we stepped back, we'd hit the wall. Fortunately for me, in those kinds of situations against the guys I played, I had pretty good adaptability; I would usually win in bad conditions.

Strangely enough, even though I couldn't get in the service because I supposedly had a weak left eye, I saw extremely well in the dark. If the lights weren't too good, it gave me an edge on my opponent. That helped me in a lot of matches on those pro tours. My weak left eye was why I couldn't get into either service. I wanted to go into the air force. I thought I'd be a damned good pilot. I ended up in the Pacific with the coast guard. It's funny that although I couldn't see well enough to fly, I could see like hell in those dark arenas.

"At one time, Wilson had sixteen different models of the Jack Kramer racket. Not only were they sold in legitimate sporting goods stores and tennis shops, they were also in Sears, Roebuck and Montgomery Ward catalogs all over the world."

—JACK KRAMER

"I played with a Jack Kramer wooden racket for years. You know what's funny? When I turned pro I signed a contract with Rawlings and all I did was paint the Kramer racket with their colors. They couldn't make a racket that was nearly as good. A lot of us did that who were under contract with other rackets. Jack probably sold another couple thousand rackets just for us pro players who didn't want to switch."

—BILLY MARTIN,
UCLA tennis coach

Robbin Adair

Tennis coach at Coronado High School, California, for thirty-five years

We went to play a high school match about 110 miles from home. We got off the bus and the girls went in to change. Suzy came back out in tears. She'd forgotten her shoes, she'd forgotten her underpants, and she'd forgotten her skirt. Typical Suzy. Here we were away from home and she didn't have any clothes to play in. We borrowed some stuff, got her covered, and she played.

That year's team won twelve matches in a row, and one of the girls said, "Coach, we're having such a great year, we've just got to bronze our shoes." At the end of that year, they spray-painted their tennis shoes bronze and put one on a plaque for each of the senior girls who was graduating, except for Suzy, who was always missing stuff. They left hers blank.

Karen Hantze Susman

Wimbledon singles and doubles champion

In 1961, Billie Jean Moffitt (King) was going to Wimbledon for the first time. I recognized Billie's tremendous volleying instincts and doubles play and asked her to be my partner. She was thrilled because I'd been to Wimbledon before and, being a year older, had a little more experience. She hadn't played as much as I had internationally so she was real excited. Of course, I was also because I just had the feeling that Billie and I could do well there with her style.

I always enjoyed Billie. She was fun on the court. We change as we get older, and it's more of a business and there's more at risk, but in the beginning, Billie was extremely fun on the court and loved being out there. She was an entertainer and I was more of the calm kind. But it was fun being with that kind of a personality. We blended well, and we both respected our doubles talent. It worked out really well.

We were bubbly, bouncy teenagers with very little worldliness in that tennis atmosphere. It was just great. To save on expenses, we stayed in a flat that was up about three stories, without a phone or bathroom in the room. Barbara, the owner of the flat, lived on the first floor. My future husband, Rod Susman, would call and the time difference would have him calling at about four in the morning. The phone would ring, Barbara would come up and get me.

We were just distractions in the beginning. But as soon as Barbara found out we were Wimbledon players and we were doing pretty well, we got better and better breakfasts as time went on. It started out as a little piece of toast with tea and became a lavish breakfast by the second week. We gave her tickets for the finals. This would be like a dream come true for someone, for anybody, but particularly for her because she loved tennis and she had never been to Wimbledon. As we left the court after winning the finals, we saw Barbara, and the expression of joy and happiness that she had on her face was priceless. She called us "her girls." We went from being zeros to tens in two weeks.

Geoff Griffin

Director of the Balboa Tennis Club in San Diego

I was so impressed with a little girl I was giving a lesson to. I was working with her volley and she was always ready. A lot of people are just never ready to hit the ball, but being ready to hit and preparing early is critical. I kept hearing her whisper the word *hiccup*. She said teaching-pro Gretchen Magers showed her the "hiccup."

When you hit the ball you say, "Hic," and when you put your racket back into a ready position you say, "Cup." This little girl was constantly hitting and putting her racket up saying, "Hiccup, hiccup," all over the court.

It made a huge difference in how she volleyed. She was always ready. I borrowed the word and now I use Gretchen's "hiccup" teaching aide in all my clinics with little kids.

"Some parents are great with the kids, winning or losing; they really teach them how to be great sports. That's what I like to see. Maybe that's not developing a champion, but I'd rather see sportsmanship than anything. Everybody likes to win, but there's a right way to do it."

—GEOFF GRIFFIN

"When I was a kid, my father always said if you're playing somebody who's not as good as you don't start to let them win; it's bad sportsmanship. You should go all out and always try to win. It's an insult to your opponent if you try to play easy."

—DICK VAN PATTEN,
star of the television show Eight Is Enough

"Dick Van Patten learned to serve in a delicatessen. He's all slices and cuts."

—BERNIE KOPELL,
star of the television series The Love Boat

"I love to play with people as good or better than me, and they're easy to find."

—ALAN THICKE,
star of the television series Growing Pains

Stan Smith

International Tennis Hall of Fame

The oddest thing happened when I was playing in Washington, D.C., at the Washington Star Tournament. It was 4–0 in the first set and deuce point. I hit a first serve about 130 mph, just as a bird flew across the court. Like a dive-bomber, it came really low, about an inch above the ground. The bird and ball collided and it ended the bird's career.

I stepped over the net, picked up the bird, and handed it to the linesman. The pay off to the story was, I had just started playing golf here at Hilton Head. The next day in the *Washington Star* newspaper, who was the sponsor of the tournament, the headline read, "Smith Gets Birdie at Washington Star."

"I used the same motion as I use on my tennis serve when I gave my famous Daniel Boone hatchet-throwing demonstration on *The Tonight Show Starring Johnny Carson.* I was right on target, a perfect ace. It led, according to the *Guinness Book of World Records,* to the longest laugh in television history."

—ED AMES,
star of the television series Daniel Boone
and outstanding vocalist

Lornie Kuhle

Owner of the Bobby Riggs Tennis Club

The one analysis I've come up with that not many people have thought about is, when Bobby Riggs played Billie Jean King, he really won the match. When you look at it, if he had actually won the match, it would have been treated in history as a nothing, as a charade, as a circus act.

But because he lost, it is now looked upon as a turning point for social change for women. It's being written about all the time, and there was also a recent television movie. It goes down in history as a milestone in women's rights.

It really was a victory. More people talk about him now than they would if he had won the whole thing. That's the funny thing. He actually ended up getting so much notoriety out of it by losing that he really came out a winner.

Todd Martin

Winner of the Association of Tennis Professionals
(ATP) Tour Sportsmanship Award, 1993 and 1994

I lost to Pete Sampras in the finals of the U.S. Open in 1993 and in the finals of the Australian Open in 1994. After the U.S. Open, I was watching the award ceremony with my mom and during it, Pete said, "Wow, I've just been working my ass off out here." I looked at my mom and I was, like, "Pete, what are you saying?"

When I lost to him the next year in the finals of Australia, I got up to receive my award and I said, "Well, we all have to give credit to Pete, because he's really been working his butt off out here." He knew what I was doing; subtly, I gave him a jab that nobody else knew I was giving him.

"You have to be extreme to be exceptional. I couldn't revel in being number one. I had to get to zero. When my fitness was at its peak, I was intimidating. I made guys cave in. They'd be dejected in the locker room after matches, and I'd go out for a run, as if it wasn't enough. I'd rub it in their faces. I meant to do that."

—JIM COURIER,
winner of four Grand Slam championships

195

Scott Bondurant

Former Stanford University tennis captain

When I was at Stanford, we were competing against USC. I had been playing pretty well and then I started to get behind. It was early in the third set, but the momentum had definitely shifted to the other side of the net.

Our coach, Dick Gould, always left me alone because I had a reasonably good handle on what I was doing. This time, though, he came out on the court and put his arm around me and said, "Scott, I've got nothing to tell you; I just want to make him think I do." I ended up winning the match. I got a big kick out of that. It worked pretty well.

Dick Gould

Stanford University tennis coach

In the early 1970s, we played our feature tennis matches indoors in Maples Pavilion, the basketball arena on the campus of Stanford. We bought a carpet, put it down, and more than 7,000 people would come to watch a college tennis match. This was really the big time. Stanford's band was there and the cheerleaders were there. The place was rocking.

My associate coach now, John Whitlinger, was playing. All of a sudden, he looked at me kind of funny. I couldn't get off the bench because a coach isn't allowed to interrupt play. John kept saying, "Coach, Coach, I've got to talk to you."

I looked at the umpire to see if I could see him for a second and he said okay. John came over and whispered, "My jockstrap broke."

The umpire gave him a time-out and he left the court and went into the locker room. Naturally, when something like that happens, the word gets around quickly. When John came back on the court, the Stanford band immediately burst into the popular song of that time, "Yellow River."

———————

Players

Players